THE
CHESTER GUIDE

THE

CHESTER GUIDE

---

by Hugh Roberts

Chester City Council

This book number is

473

of a limited edition of 500 copies

First published 1851
This edition specially produced by
Shawn Stipling
for the publisher
Chester Archives
Chester City Council
1996

ISBN 1 872587 08 9

Printed in Great Britain by
Bemrose Shafron Printers Ltd.

FOREWORD

By the late 18th century, Chester was becoming a popular place to visit. Many stagecoach services ran to and from London, the Midlands and the South-West. Over 100 inns and public houses provided hospitality. To meet the needs of visitors and to encourage more, booksellers and printers started producing guidebooks. The first of these was Peter Broster's, *Chester Guide and Directory* (1781), which ran to several editions. Later guides included James Hanshall's, *The Stranger in Chester* (1816), John Seacome's, *Chester Guide* (1836), and Joseph Hemingway's, *Panorama of the City of Chester* (1836).

The coming of the railways to Chester in 1840 brought yet more visitors, especially after the present General Station was opened in 1848. Chester became a major regional railway centre, serving 2000 passengers each day, and new hotels were opened to meet growing visitor demands.

Hugh Roberts was a printer and bookseller, with a printing works in Eastgate Row. Originally in business by himself, he joined with George Prichard in 1853. Prichard had issued a similar version of the *Chester Guide* under his own imprint, c. 1852. They traded as Prichard, Roberts and Company, but around 1857, George Prichard left to join another firm. Hugh Roberts continued on his own and produced a second edition of his Chester Guide in 1858. His business was split up in 1864. John Phillipson bought out his book selling business and his printing and bookbinding plant was acquired by the firm, W.F. and M. Healey.

Hugh Roberts' guidebook laid much of the groundwork for Thomas Hughes', *Stranger's Handbook to Chester*, first published in 1856. The tradition of producing illustrated guidebooks for visitors has continued down to the present day.

THE

CHESTER GUIDE:

CONTAINING

A COPIOUS HISTORY OF THE ANTIQUITIES AND PUBLIC
BUILDINGS OF THE CITY,

AND

A Descriptive Account of Eaton Hall.

WITH TWENTY-EIGHT ILLUSTRATIONS.

CHESTER:

H. ROBERTS, PRINTER AND BOOKSELLER.
SOLD BY ALL BOOKSELLERS.

THE ANCIENT HISTORY

OF

THE CITY OF CHESTER.

HERE are but few places in the kingdom, if indeed there are any, that can present such varied attractions to the mind of an antiquary as this ancient city. It is rich in memorable incidents and associations. It has a history chronicled not only in books, but in its walls, towers, rows, and venerable remains; all of which to an intelligent and inquiring mind, are suggestive of much respecting the people and times of the eventful past.

A close investigation into the ancient history of Chester is not only interesting, as throwing considerable light on the varied agencies which have contributed to its rise and progress;—exhibiting the sort of antecedents out of which its present has sprung;—but also as furnishing most valuable facts elucidatory of our national annals. Chester has been from time to time the theatre of momentous events, bearing on the development of our national institutions, liberties, and laws. Its history, therefore, cannot fail of interest to the thoughtful, who will gladly welcome any light that can be thrown on the progress of any portion of their country.

The origin of Chester is of very remote date. No definite conclusion has been reached respecting the exact time of its foundation. Various hypotheses have been started, some of them grotesque and ridiculous enough, but it appears to be lost in extreme remoteness.

All writers of note who have investigated the question with great painstaking and ability, concur in the acknowledgment of its great antiquity, and indeed, it is at once a result and a proof of its very early origin, that wo have had so many curious conjectures and ingenious theories on the subject. There are some sensible remarks on this point in "King's Vale Royal," which we cannot refrain from transcribing for the benefit of

A

the reader. "That there hath been so much wrestling and striving to find out the ancient names and the first original of the City of Chester, is to me one argument of the ancientness thereof; for there is no certainty known, how can it be but beyond the reach of all intelligence, that the laborious writers of all ages have endeavoured after. Whereupon I hold it for a conclusion that many monuments in this kingdom, whereof there can be found no memory of their foundation, are more ancient than those which have their foundations either certainly known or probably conjectured.

Although for my part I see not but very weak grounds for these conjectures, who would bring our City of Chester's foundation from beyond all possibility of record, yet I will not prejudicate any in their surmises, nor defraud them of the praises that any shall think good to bestow upon those who have laboured in collections of that kind.

The first name that I find this city to have been supposed to have bourne, was Neomagus ; and this they derive from Magus, the son of Samothes, who was the first planter of inhabitants in this isle after Noah's flood, which now containeth England, Scotland, and Wales ; and of him was called Samothea ; and this Samothes was son to Japhet, the third son of Noah and of this Magus, who first built a city even in this place or near unto it, as it is supposed, the same was called Neomagus. This conjecture I find observed by the learned Sir Thomas Elliott, who saith directly that Neomagus stood where Chester now standeth. Whether it carried ·that name for any long time of continuance, or when it lost the same, I find no certainty. Randulphus, a monk of Chester, and another of the old Polychronicon, hath another foundation from a giant forsooth called Leon Gower, which Gower Marius calls the vanquisher of the Picts, who laid the first foundation of this city, as it were, in a kind of rude and disordered fashion, which afterwards by Leir, King of Britain, was brought to a more pleasant fashion of building, which is best expressed in the verses of Henry Bradshaw, another monk of Chester, who writ the life of St. Werburgh, and therein these verses :—

> "The founder of this city, as saith Polychronicon,
> Was Leon Gower, a mighty strong giant;
> Which builded caves and dungeons many a one,
> No goodly buildings, no proper, no pleasant.
> But King Leir, a Briton fine and valiant,
> Was founder of Chester by pleasant building,
> And was named Guer Leir by the king."

Touching which foundation, supposed by this Leon Gower, I do, by so much less, give approbation; by how much methinks that opinion of Mr. Camden's seems most probable, drawn from the ancient British language, of whom it hath been called Caerlegian Caerleon vaur Caerleon or Dufyrdwy, as the Britons called it; which names are derived from that legion of the Romans, called Vicessima Victrix, which where first planted here in the second consulship of Galba, with Titus Vincus; and afterwards established under the government of Julius Agricola appointed by this city, &c. By whom, or howsoever, the same city had her first foundation, it is manifest enough that it is exceeding antient; and even the doubtfulness of the first foundation makes it, as before I touched, of undoubted antiquity."

It is quite clear as an authenticated matter of fact, that Chester was in very early possession of the Romans. It was the head quarters of the 20th legion, which, we find, came into Britain before the year 61; for it had a share in the defeat of Boadicea by Suetonius. After that important victory this mighty and intrepid people marched onward towards North Wales, and established their authority in Cheshire.

Scattered through the city, have been discovered many vestiges of their power, which enable us to trace their history with considerable distinctness. Wherever they planted their potent sway, they left behind permanent records of their greatness and skill. Many of these memorials have been discovered in various parts of the old city, and we are glad to find that through the intelligent and zealous investigations of the Chester Archœological Society, these antiquities are now made tributary to the enlightenment and instruction of the inhabitants respecting the history of their own locality.

Not only by the antiquarian, however, is Chester worthy of attention; there is scarcely any order of mind or taste, but may here find its fitting gratification. Its noble arched bridge, venerable cathedral, unique rows, and walls encompassing the city, with a considerable number and variety of relics, all combine to make Chester a locality the most precious in treasures of investigation, that can be found in the kingdom. It is the metropolis of the county palatine of that name, and is pleasantly situated above the river Dee, on a rising ground. Its names have been various. Its Roman name is Deva, undoubtedly because of its being situated on the river Dee. Then Cestriæ, from Castrum "camp;" and Castrum Legionis, "the Camp of the Legion." Its British names were Caer Lleon—"the Camp of the Legion;" and Caer Lleon Vawr, or Ddyfrdwy, "the Camp of the Great Legion on the Dee."

During the brilliant lieutenancy of Julius Agricola, A.D. 85, it became a 'Roman colony; and the place was called from them and from its situation, Colonia Devana. This is clearly demonstrated by a coin of Septimus Geta, son of Severus, which has this inscription—

Col. Devana. Leg. xx. Victrix.

For two or three centuries after this Chester appears to have continued undisturbed in the power of the Romans ; during which period "it was a centre of operations while conquest was being produced ; a centre of civilization and commercial intercourse when the dominion of the empire was established. The actual form of the city, its division by streets into four quarters, exhibits the arrangement which the Romans established in their camp, and which they naturally transferred to the cities which took the place of their military stations. Traces of the work of that wonderful people still remain on our walls, and on the rocky brows which surround them ; and excite the attention and reward the diligence of the antiquarian. Those pigs of lead, the produce of Roman industry, which are first mentioned in "Camden's Britannia," as being found in the neighbourhood of Chester, and two of which have recently been discovered, are memorials of the early period at which the mineral wealth of this district was known, and of the commerce to which it gave rise." It is a fact, clearly established by history, that to the Romans we are greatly indebted for the introduction of a much higher order of civilization than that which they found existing when they took possession of the country. They were the pioneers of social and religious progress. Previous to the Roman invasion, the inhabitants were unacquainted with the laws and arts of civilized life ; —painted their bodies,—despised the institution of marriage,— clothed themselves in skins—knew very little of agriculture— were furious in disposition, and cruel in their religious superstitions. We find that the practice of human sacrifices was very general amongst them, and in every respect their social and moral condition rude and barbarous in the extreme. So wedded were they to their idolatrous worship and cruel rites, that the Romans after their conquest, found it necessary to abolish their religion by penal statutes : an exercise of power which was not usual with these tolerating conquerors. About the year 50, the Emperor Claudius Cæsar, subdued the greater part of Britain, and received the submission of several of the British states who inhabited the south east part of the Island. The other Britons under the command of Caractacus, still maintained an obstinate resistance, and the Romans made little progress against them, until Ostorius Scapula was sent over in the year 50, to command their armies. This renowned general found the country in a state of great excitement and dissatisfaction, but speedily advanced the Roman conquests over the Britons—defeated

Caractacus in a great battle—took him prisoner, and sent him to Rome—where his magnanimous behaviour procured him better treatment than those conquerors usually bestowed on native princes. He pardoned Caractacus and his family, and commanded that their chains should immediately be taken off.

Hollingshed is of opinion that Ostorius Scapula was the founder of Chester, and the reasons he adduces are certainly possessed of great force. He says, "It is not unlike that it might be first built by P. Ostorius Scapula, who, as we find, after he had subdued Caractacus, King of the Ordonices, that inhabited the countries now called Lancashire, Cheshire, and Salopshire, built in those parts, and among the Silures, certeine places of defense, for the better harbrough of his men of warre, and keeping downe of such Britaines as were still readie to move rebellion."

Passing over the space of a few years, we find Julius Agricola completing the conquest of this Island. Such was his formidable power and skilful policy in governing the people, that we are told they soon became reconciled to the supremacy of the Roman arms and language. He quelled their animosity to the Roman yoke, and certainly did very much for the progress of the people in civilization, knowledge, and the arts of peace.

There is perhaps no place in the kingdom that can boast of so many monuments of Roman skill and ingenuity as our own venerable city ; but as these will be described in detail as we proceed we will not stay to specify them here.

About the year 448 the Romans withdrew from the Island after having been masters of the most considerable part of its territory for nearly four centuries, and left the Britons to arm for their own defence. But from their long subjection to a foreign yoke, they had lost that desperate valor and love of independence which had before been prominent features of their character, and were but in a sorry condition to resist the aggression of a formidable foe. No sooner, therefore, had the Romans withdrawn their troops, than the Scots and Picts invaded the country with their terrible forces, and spread devastation and ruin along the line of their march. These vindictive and rapacious barbarians, fired with the lust of conquest, made a pitiless onslaught upon the property and lives of the people. The unhappy Britons petitioned, without effect, for the interposition of Rome, which had declared its resolution for ever to abandon them. The British ambassadors were entrusted with a letter to the legate at Rome, pathetically stating their perilous dilemma, and invoking their immediate aid. The tenor of the epistle, which was inscribed "the groans of the Britons," certainly was in perfect keeping with the quaint but expressive inscription :—

" The barbarians, on the one hand, chase us unto the sea ;
the sea, on the other, throws us back upon the barbarians ;
and we have only the hard choice left us of perishing by the
sword or by the waves."

The intestine commotions which were then shaking the Roman
empire to its centre, prevented the masters of the then world
from affording the timely aid sought at their hands.

The petition of the Britons being thus rejected,—their hope
of re-inforcement suddenly blighted,—a panic soon spread itself
amongst the troops, which reduced them to a state of despair.
Dispirited and undisciplined, conquered already by fear, they
were unequal to a conflict with their much dreaded foes. They
therefore deserted their habitations, and fled for refuge into
the forests and mountains, where they suffered alike from the
inroads of hunger and their enemy. Their miserable condition
and sufferings are described by early chroniclers as desperate
in the extreme. We are told that the barbarian invaders not
being fully prepared for the permanent occupancy of the country
which they had ravaged, and being harrassed by the dispersed
Britons, who had not dared to resist them in a body, they
retreated with the spoils unto their own country.

The Britons taking advantage of this cessation of hostilities,
returned to their usual occupations, and soon recovered considerable prosperity. But as a striking illustration of their im-
providence, and utter ignorance of the tactics of war, during
the interval they exercised no forethought, did not attempt to
recruit their strength, or make any further provision for the
resistance of the enemy, who soon therefore threatened them
with a new invasion.

Despairing of any re-inforcement from Rome, they now invoked the aid of the Saxons, who promptly complied with the
invitation, and under Hengist and Horsa, two Saxon chiefs,
who were also brothers, soon wrested Chester from the hands
of the invaders. The Saxons perceiving the weakness of the
degenerate allies, soon began to entertain the project of con-
quering them, and seizing the country as their spoil. During
the conflict which ensued between the Britons and Saxons, who
from allies became masters, Chester was frequently taken and
re-taken, and suffered severely in various sieges.   Ultimately,
the Aborigines were totally subjugated under the mightier sway
of Saxon arms.

In 607, Ethelfred, king of Northumbria, waged a sanguinary
battle with the Britons under the walls of Chester, whom he
defeated.

It is recorded that he came to avenge the quarrel of St. Augustine, whose metropolitan jurisdiction the British monks refused

to admit. Augustine is said to have denounced against them the vengeance of heaven, for this reason, three years previously.

Sammes, in his Antiquities of Britain, gives an interesting statement of this celebrated battle, "Edelfrid, the strongest King of the English, having gathered together a great army about the city of Chester, he made a great slaughter of that nation; but when he was going to give the onset, he espied priests and others, who were come thither to entreat God for the success of the army, standing apart in a place of advantage; he asked who they were, and for what purpose they had met there? When Edelfrid had understood the cause of their coming, he said, "If, therefore, they cry unto their God against us, certainly they, although they bear no arms, fight against us, who prosecute us by their prayers."

The victory was not destined, however, to be an abiding one. The supremacy of Ethelfrid over the Britons was not long in duration. History tells us that a few years after he had achieved his conquest, the united forces of Brocmail and three other British princes, rescued from his hands the possession of Chester, and put his armies to flight. In 613, the Britons assembled in Chester and elected Cadwon their king, who reigned with great honor for twenty-two years.

From this period to the close of the Heptarchy, we have but very scanty materials respecting the history of Chester. The Britons appear to have retained possession of it until about the year 828, when it was finally taken out of their hands by Egbert, during the reign of the British prince Mervyn and his wife Esylht.

In a few years afterwards (894 or 895), the city underwent a heavy calamity from its invasion by Harold, king of the Danes, Mancolin, king of the Scots, and another confederate prince, who are said to have encamped on Hoole heath, near Chester, and, after a long siege, reduced the city. These predatory pirates were soon after attacked and conquered by Alfred, who utterly routed them from the military defences in which they had embosomed themselves, and destroyed all the cattle and corn of the district. Although historians are not agreed as the exact date when this took place, yet the result appears to be that, after a temporary possession, they were compelled by famine suddenly to depart and take their course through North Wales.

After the evacuation of the city by the Danes, it remained in ruins until about the year 908, when it was restored by Ethelred, the first Earl of Mercia, and Ethelfled his wife, who, it is said, enlarged it to double the extent of the Roman town. Sir Peter Leycester says that "Ethelred and his countess

restored Caerleon, that is Legecestria, now called Chester, after
it was destroyed by the Danes, and enclosed it with new walls,
and made it nigh such two as it was before; so that the castle
that was sometime by the water without the walls, is now
in the town within the walls." All the narratives which
have been handed down to us of this celebrated woman, represent her as possessed of incomparable talent, great enterprize, and pure mind. She employed the great power and
opportunity she possessed with admirable wisdom, and made
them subservient to acts of munificence and piety. She died
at Tamworth in 922, from whence her body was translated
to Gloucester. Leycester gives a lengthy record of her good
deeds, which prepares us for the fact that her loss was deeply
and universally regretted throughout the whole kingdom.

The security of Chester against the Danish invaders was
ultimately effected by the victories of Edmund, in or about
942, after which it was occasionally honoured by the residence of the Saxon sovereigns. Pennant says King Edgar
made this one of the stations in his annual circum-navigation
of his dominions. About the year 973, he visited Chester, attended by his court, and received the homage of his vassal
kings. It is said that one day entering his barge, he assumed
the helm, and made his eight tributary princes row him from
the palace which stood in the field at Handbridge, opposite
the prison wards of the castle, and which still bears his
name, up the river Dee as far as the monastery of St. John's.
In the following century Chester was possessed by the Earls
of Mercia until the Norman Conquest in 1066. The tyranny,
violence, and bloodshed which marked the course of William
the Conqueror, met with determined resistance in various
parts of the country; but in the course of six or seven years
he utterly crushed all opposition, and became absolute master
of the island. He introduced into England the feudal system "with its military, aristocracy, its pride, its splendour,
and its iron dominion. The importance of Chester as a military station, was shewn by its being assigned as a fief to one
of the chief leaders in the Norman army, and on his death
by its being given to the nephew of the Duke himself, under
whom it was invested with privileges which raised it almost
to the rank of a separate principality. Under Hugh, the first
Earl of Chester, and his immediate successors, we may suppose that most of those castles were built, which form objects
of antiquarian research in the neighbourhood, but which are
melancholy records of the state of society at the time, since
they were evidently built to protect the frontiers from the
continued invasions of the Welsh. Some of these still re-

main; and from their extent and magnificence, appear to have been the residences of the Earls themselves. Many more have perished, and can only be traced by the banks which mark the outline of their plan. These were probably of an inferior description, and are rather to be considered as guard-houses for the protection of some particular pass, than as regular fortresses. There are traces of this kind at Doddleston, at Pulford, at Aldford, at Holt, at Shotwick, beside the larger and more distinguished holds at Beeston, Halton, Chester, and Hawarden; and probably few years passed but that some inroad of the Welsh carried fire and slaughter to the very gates of Chester, and swept the cattle and produce from the fields." *

For many years previous to the Norman Conquest, Chester was governed by Dukes or Earls; but William, perceiving the danger of entrusting so large a territory in the hands of any one of his barons, curtailed the provinces within narrower limits, and thereby crippled the power which had often proved dangerous to the throne, and at the same time augmented his own, by having a larger number of gifts and emoluments to bestow on his followers. In the first instance, William gave Cheshire to Gherbodus, a noble Fleming, who, having obtained permission of the king to visit Flanders for the transaction of some private business, there fell into the hands of his enemies, and was obliged to resign the earldom to Hugh Lupus, the nephew of the Conqueror, who was appointed in his stead. The Earldom was now erected into a Palatinate. Camden says "William the 1st created Hugh, surnamed Lupus, the 1st Earl of Chester and Count Palatine, and gave unto him and his heirs all the county, to be holden as freely by the sword as the king himself held England by his crown."

By reason of this grant the Earls of Chester were invested with sovereign jurisdiction, and held their own parliaments. It has been supposed probable that Lupus was invested with his new dignity at Chester by William himself, when he was present here in person in 1069.

He created several barons to assist him in his council and government, some of whom we find upon record, as Nigel, Baron of Halton; Sir William Maldebeng, of Malbanc, Baron of Wich Malbanc, or Nantwich; Richard de Vernon, Baron of Shipbroke; Gilbert Venables, Baron of Kinderton; Hamon de Massey, Baron of Dunham Massey; Warren de Poynton, Baron of Stockport; Eustace de Monthalt, Baron of Monthalt.

* Rev. Chancellor Raikes' Introductory Lecture before the Chester Archæological Society.

He converted the church of St. Werburgh into an abbey, by the advice of St. Anselm.

He continued earl thirty-one years, died the 27th of July, 1101, and was buried in the church yard, but afterwards removed to the present Chapter-house of the Cathedral, where his body was found in 1724, wrapped in leather, enclosed in a stone coffin; at the head of the coffin was a stone in the shape of a T, with a wolf's head, the arms which he bore, being engraven upon it.

His Sword of Dignity forms one of the many valuable curiosities preserved in the British Museum. It is about four feet long, and so unwieldy as to require considerable strength to brandish it with both hands. His parliament was formed of eight barons, who were obliged to attend him. Every baron had four esquires; every esquire one gentleman, and every gentleman one valet. The barons had the power of life and death. Hugh Lupus was succeeded by his son Richard, who was drowned in his passage from Normandy. He governed nineteen years, and was succeeded by Ranulph, surnamed *Mechines*, son of Margaret, sister to Lupus. Ranulph died at Chester A.D. 1129,* and was succeeded by the heroic Ranulph II., surnamed *Geronjis*, who, having held the Earldom twenty-five years, he was poisoned in 1153, and was as buried at Chester.

Hugh II. his son, surnamed Cyvelioc, succeeded him, and continued in the Earldom twenty-eight years. He died at Leeke, in Staffordshire, and was buried at Chester.

Hugh was succeeded by his son Ranulph, surnamed *Blundeville*, who, for his benevolence, was styled *Ranulph the Good*. He served in the holy wars, and was as celebrated as any of the Seven Champions of Christendom. After his return he built Beeston Castle, in this county; a noble and imposing fortress which, before the use of fire-arms, might have been deemed impregnable. It is built on an insulated rock, and its summit is one hundred yards above the level of the brook that runs at its base. It endured three sieges during the civil wars. The middle part of the slope is surrounded by towers, which time, however, has dismantled; the well in the upper part was cut through the rock to the depth of one hundred yards, in the course of time, it became nearly filled up with rubbish, but within the last few years was cleared, built round, and enclosed, by J. Tollemache, Esq., M.P., to whom the castle belongs.

---

* This Earl was the first who assumed the present arms of Chester: three wheat sheaves in a field azure.

This Earl Ranulph was besieged by the Welsh in the castle of Rhudlan, and was relieved by Ralph Dutton, son-in-law of Roger Lacy, Constable of Chester, at the head of a large body of fiddlers, minstrels, &c., who were then assembled at the fair of Hugh Lupus. A remarkable privilege of this fair was, that no thief or malefactor that attended it, should be attached or punished, except for offences then and there committed. With this motley crew, Dutton marched into Wales, and raised the siege; for which Ranulph rewarded him with full power over all the instruments of his preservation, and the privilege of licensing the minstrels; in virtue whereof Dutton's heirs claimed from the minstrels four bottles of wine and one lance, with a fee of fourpence-halfpenny; and from every courtezan in the city and county, "officium suum exercens," fourpence. The anniversary of the above narrated achievement was formerly celebrated annually, on the festival of St. John the Baptist, by a regular procession of the minstrels to the church of their tutelar saint in this city, St. Werburgh, in honour of whom Hugh Lupus granted to the minstrels, &c. the above mentioned privilege, which is recognised in all subsequent vagrant acts, by a special exception in favour of the minstrel jurisdiction of the Duttons, of Dutton, in Cheshire. This last Earl Ranulph died in 1232, and was buried at Chester.

John Scott succeeded Ranulph, who died without issue, not without suspicion, Leycester says, of being poisoned by the contrivance of Helene his wife.

The Earls of Chester continued to exercise their local sovereignty for about one hundred and sixty years. They held that sovereignty, it is true, as the representatives of the paramount sovereignty of the King of England, and as owing allegiance to him in all things; but so far as the government of the Palatinate was concerned, their rule, though nominally mediate, was actually absolute, for the King does not appear to have thwarted their jurisdiction, or in any way to have exerted his supreme authority, beyond the retaining a mint at Chester.

After the death of the seventh Earl in 1237, Henry the Third united the Earldom to the Crown; he afterwards conferred it upon his eldest son, Prince Edward, about A.D. 1245, who, two years after this, received the homage of his military tenants at Chester. From that period to the present the title of Earl of Chester has been vested in the eldest son of the reigning sovereign, and is now held by his Royal Highness Albert Prince of Wales.

In 1255 Llewellyn ap Gryffid, Prince of Wales, provoked

by the cruel injuries his subjects had received from Geffrey Langley, Lieutenant of the County under Prince Edward, carried fire and sword to the gates of Chester. In 1257 Henry the Third summoned his nobility and bishops to attend, with their vassals, at Chester, in order to invade Wales; and in 1275 Edward the First appointed the city as the place for Llewelyn to do him homage, whose refusal ended with the ruin of himself and his principality; for in 1300 Edward of Carnarvon here received the final acknowledgment of the Welsh to the sovereignty of England; and in a few years afterwards, Llewellyn was brought hither a prisoner from Flint castle. Richard the Second visited this his favourite city in 1397, and in 1399 he was brought a prisoner from Flint castle to the castle of Chester, which Henry the Fourth had seized, and put to death many of his adherents.

In Owen Glendower's wars, this city was a *place d'armes* for the English troops in the expeditions against the Welsh, who, ever tenacious of their independence, were as unwilling to submit to the Norman as the Saxon yoke.

In 1459, Henry the Sixth with Queen Margaret, and her son Edward, visited Chester, and bestowed little silver swans on the Cheshire gentlemen who espoused her cause.

It appears that Henry the Seventh and his Queen also visited Chester in 1493. In 1554 George Marsh, the unflinching martyr, was publicly burnt at Boughton, for his stedfast adherence to the Protestant faith. He sacrificed his life rather than falsify his conscience, or recant his faith. In the year 1617 the city was honoured with the presence of James the First, when Edward Button, the then Mayor, presented the King with a gilt cup containing one hundred jacobuses of gold.

From this time no event of any great importance appears to have transpired, until the city was involved in the calamities of a siege, in consequence of its loyalty to Charles the First. The city stood the siege for some months; but the inhabitants at last, reduced to the extremity of famine, so that they were compelled to eat horses, dogs, cats, and other animals, abandoned their resistance, and yielded the city on February the 3rd, 1645-6.

Chester was, probably, in the time of the Romans, or earlier, a thriving port. The Saxon navy was stationed here, and it was also the seat of the Mercian Kings. About the time of the Conquest, the imports and exports appear to have been considerable. But as an illustration of the barbarism of the times, we may just mention, that one article of the latter was slaves, obtained, it is conjectured, from the captives which were made in the frequent wars with the Welsh. It is quite clear that Chester was, in former times, a busy and flourishing port, because of the perfectly navigable condition of the Dee. All the early writers of its history unite in bearing testimony to this point. It may here be just mentioned as a curious and interesting fact, that some centuries ago, Flookersbrook was covered over with water, and that a deep and broad channel flowed through Mollington, Stanney, and that direction, which emptied itself into the estuary now called the Mersey. Hollinshed, after tracing minutely the course of the Dee through Flookersbrook up to Stanney, distinctly states that it "sendeth foorth one arme by Stannie Poole, and the Parke side into Merseie arme," &c. Speed distinctly marks out this course in his map; and it is still more broadly defined in an old Dutch map, which we have recently seen, of a much earlier date, printed at Rotterdam.

In consequence of the uncertain and imperfect state of the river, the once thriving commerce of this ancient port has dwindled into insignificance, and Liverpool has reaped the advantage. Spirited efforts are now being made to deepen the channel of the river, so as to render it navigable by vessels of heavy burden. A bill is now before parliament for the purpose of securing this most desirable consummation.

THE ANCIENT BRITISH CHURCH.

 SHORT inquiry into the history of the British Church may, perhaps, be acceptable to those who are interested in such investigations. It is utterly beyond our power to contribute anything new in the much and long-disputed question of the first introduction of Christianity into England, or adduce any additional materiél, or employ any novel argument which would in the least aid in deciding the controverted point. It is quite clear, however, that very early in the Christian era, sometime during the 1st century, the light of Christian truth penetrated into this Island. Many conflicting theories have been propounded as to the chronology and the agent employed by Divine Providence, in conferring this great boon upon our country; but as all the varied traditions seem to point to the Apostolic age, we may the more readily acquiesce in the loss of not knowing *who* was the actual instrument, especially when we remember, how many of the world's greatest benefactors have been unknown to those who are most indebted to them.

The foundation of the Church in Britain has been ascribed, by many eminent authorities, to St Paul; and the learned Dr. Burgess, Bishop of St. David's, goes so far as to say, that this interesting point is established by as much substantial evidence as any historical fact can require; and he proceeds to give the testimony of the first six centuries in support of the doctrine. The first and most important testimony is that of Clemens Romanus, "the intimate friend and fellow-labourer of St. Paul," who says, that in preaching the gospel the apostles went *to the utmost bounds of the west,* which seems to have been the usual designation of Britain. Theoderet speaks of the inhabitants of Spain, Gaul, and *Britain,* as dwelling in the *utmost bounds of the west.* In the second century, Irenæus speaks of Christianity as propagated to the utmost bounds of the earth by the apostles and their disciples; and Tertullian, at the beginning of the third century, gives a kindred testimony. In the fourth century, (A.D. 270-340) Eusebius says, that some of the apostles passed over the ocean to the British Isles; and Jerome, in the same century, ascribes this province to St. Paul, and says, that after his imprisonment, having been in Spain, he went from ocean to ocean, and preached the gospel in the *western parts.* Theoderet, in the fifth century, and Venantius Fortunatus in the sixth, are also quoted as witnesses to the same effect.

Gildas, a Briton, called the wise, very positively ascribes the first mission to Britain to St. Joseph of Arimathea, who, according to his account, evangelized Gaul. This opinion is supported by Bede, William of Malmesbury, and many eminent divines of the Church.

Sammes, in his 'Antiquities of Britain,' inclines to the same idea, and gives an illustration of the first church supposed to be built by him; but it does not appear to be based upon sufficient evidence to entitle it to acceptance.

The conversion of Britain to the Christian faith has also been ascribed to St. Peter, St. James the Great, and to Simon Zelotes. Bishop Taylor and Dr. Cox are disposed to award the honour to the latter. Southey is of opinion that the Gospel was first introduced here by the family of Caractacus, who propagated it among the British tribes; and he is certainly upheld in this by many weighty considerations.

As there is existing such contrariety of belief among those master intellects, who have deeply studied the subject, we should certainly regard it as vain presumption to record any dogmatic judgment. At first the progress of Christianity was slow, but on that account the more sure, as it was gradually supplanting the deep-rooted prejudices of the people.   Early in the fourth century, its diffusion had become so accelerated, that Maximius and Galerius, themselves bigoted Pagans, recommended to the Emperor Diocletian the enforcement of extreme measures, in order to crush the growing religion, and the ever-memorable persecution under his reign was the result, when Christians were indiscriminately slaughtered, and churches wantonly destroyed.

Under the empire of his successor, Constantine, persecution was extinguished; churches were re-built, the offices of religion generally resumed, and the people enjoyed more than fifty years' tranquility.   In the month of August, 314, the celebrated Council of Arles was assembled; and in the lists of the ecclesiastics who attended the council, we have the names of the British Bishops,—a convincing proof this, that the Christian faith had obtained a strong hold on the minds of the people. At a council held at Ariminum, or Rimini, on the coast of the Adriatic, in 359 A.D. in reference to the Arian heresy, that was then rending the Church asunder, we find that there were assembled more than 400 Bishops, "those chiefly of the western church." Of these ecclesiastics several came from Britain, as we learn from a passage in Sulpicius Severus, which is to the effect, that three out of the eight or ten of the bishops who came from Britain, unable to pay out of their own funds the expenses occasioned by their protracted stay at Rimini, had recourse to the public allowance provided for the purpose. The bishops, upon their return to Britain, found the northern part of the Island in a distracted condition, from the destructive invasion of the Scots and Picts.

The Gospel flourished a long period in England before it was introduced into Scotland or Ireland, or even into the Principality. It is recorded by Spelman, that Wales was converted to the Christian faith about the time of the council of Arles.

While Britain continued a Roman province, Christianity continued to flourish and extend its dominion throughout the length and breadth of the land. And the Christian Britons sought not only to permeate their own Island with the influence of the truth, but in obedience to that expansive principle which it always implants, they sounded out "the word" to their Pagan neighbours in Scotland and Ireland, amongst whom we find the Britons introduced the Christian religion.   The Britons maintained their religion in their respective localities until, by the invasion of the Pagan Saxons, British Christians were exposed to persecutions almost as severe as the Diocletian period. In many places churches were destroyed or alienated to Pagan worship, and most of the clergy with their flocks, were compelled to fly for safety into Wales. Notwithstanding the sufferings by which our forefathers, at this era, were exercised, they still remained faithful to their principles, and continued to worship and receive the instructions of their ministers, according to their own faith.

In the year 490 Dubricius was elevated to the Archbishopric of Caerleon, which he appears to have held, together with the Bishopric of Llandaff. Although faithful and laborious in the discharge of the sacred duties of his primacy, we find the Pelagian heresy breaking out and making rapid progress among the Britons, disturbing the peace and unity of the church. With a view to suppress this heresy, a synod of the bishops and clergy was convened, which assembled accordingly in the year 519 at a place called Brevi (afterwards Llandewi Brevi) in Cardiganshire. Before the synod was dissolved, the age and infirmities of Dubricius induced him to resign the Archbishopric, to which St. David was unanimously appointed.

Want of space prevents our narrating the incidents which fill up the interval of church history from the time of St. David to the mission of Augustine to this country; we therefore will proceed briefly to notice that interesting and eventful enterprize. Augustine and his associates landed in Thanet A.D. 596, and in a short time after his arrival was admitted to an audience with the King, who gave them full liberty to preach their doctrines in the country, and appropriated the British church in Canterbury for their service. It has been very generally stated that the conversion of the Anglo-Saxons was by the instrumentality of the Roman missionary, but the claim is not proved by satisfactory evidence. There seems to be no doubt that they were partially instructed in the Christian faith before the visit of Augustine to our shores. When he entertained the ambitious project, however of subjecting the British to the Roman see, and also his own metropolitan jurisdiction, he was confronted with a determined resistance from the British monks, who positively refused to concede their independence, and were "fixed in the determination not to be subjugated by any foreign prince, power, or prelate." Spelman says that the Britons "stiffly opposed" the demands of Augustine to obey the Bishop of Rome and receive the Romish ceremonies; "and after the business had been a long time controverted on both sides, another synod or session was agreed on, when a great number of the British clergy were present: amongst them seven bishops. The old controversy is again renewed, but when Augustine found that he was likely to gain no farther, he desired they would but conform to him and the Romans in three things only :—

1st. In the observation of Easter.

2d. In the administration of Baptism.

3d. In assisting him with their preaching to the English Saxons. But they, suspecting the pride of Augustine, would not condescend to him in these things neither."

Failing in this first attempt to bring the monks to the recognition of his supremacy, a second synod was summoned, and the proposal already made was repeated, to which "they made answer that they would do none of these things, neither would they acknowledge him for an archbishop." All his attempts to subdue the steady resolution of the old Britons were unavailing, feuds and wars of religious bigotry ensued, and the massacre of the Bangor monks, at the battle of Chester, was the result, which we have already described.

Theodore appears to have been the first Anglo-Saxon primate. He was ordained at Rome, A.D. 669, and to his authority the British clergy submitted.

According to King's 'Vale Royal,' Theodore appointed St. Chad the first Bishop of Chester, who fixed his seat at Lichfield. "After him one Winifred was bishop, who, for his disobedience in some points, was deprived by Theodore, who appointed in his place one Sexulph. The said Theodore, by authority of a synod held at Hatfield, did divide the province of Mercia into five bishoprics, that is to say, Chester, Worcester, Lichfield, Cederna in Lindsey, and Dorchester, which after was translated to Lincoln. After Sexulf, one Aldwin was bishop of Lichfield, and next to him Eudulfus, who was adorned with the Archbishop's pall, having all the bishops under King Offa's dominions suffragans to him."

The diocese of Chester seems to have continued one with that of Lichfield to the time of the Conquest, when Pennant says a Bishop of Lichfield of the name of Peter, in the year 1075, removed his episcopal seat to Chester; and during his life made use of the monastery of St. John's for his cathedral.

His successor was Robert of Lindsey, chaplain of Wm. Rufus, who removed the see to Coventry; St. John's church, however, continued collegiate up to the time of the Reformation, at which period it had a dean, eight canons or prebends, and ten vicars choral. The prelate and his successors, although having seats at Lichfield and Coventry, as well as Chester, continued to have the designation of Bishop of Chester, until the appointment of John Ketterich, in 1415, who was not so styled, nor any of his successors until the time of the Reformation.

B

" The bishops that were before that time (although they were commonly called bishops of Chester) were bishops of Lichfield, and had but their seat or most abiding in Chester." Henry the Eight erected Chester into a distinct diocese in the 33rd year of his reign, " turning the monastery of St. Werburgh into the bishop's palace ; unto which jurisdiction was allotted Cheshire, Lancashire, Richmondshire, and part of Cumberland ; and was appointed to be within the province of York."

John Bird, D.D. " formerly a fryer of the order of the Carmelites, was the first bishop of this new foundation." He was deprived of his bishopric by Queen Mary, A.D. 1544, because of his adhesion to the Protestant faith. He was succeeded by George Cotes, who survived his consecration only about two years. He died at Chester, and was buried in the Cathedral near the bishop's throne. His memory is stained with the blood of George Marsh, who, during his episcopate, suffered martyrdom at Boughton. The next bishop was Cuthbert Scott, who was vice-chancellor of Oxford in 1554 and 1555, one of the delegates commissioned by Cardinal Pole to visit that University, and one of the four bishops who, with as many divines, undertook to defend the Church of Rome against an equal number of reformed divines. He was deposed by Queen Elizabeth, for some abusive expressions uttered against Her Majesty. William Downham, chaplain to Queen Elizabeth before she came to the crown, was consecrated Bishop of Chester, A.D. 1561. He died Nov. 1577, and was buried in the choir of the Cathedral, having sat bishop sixteen years and a half : from that time to the present there has been a regular succession of Protestant bishops.

John Graham, D. D. formerly Master of Christ's College, Cambridge, was consecrated to the see of Chester in 1848, and is at present fulfilling the duties of his high vocation with pious earnestness and diligence.

GOVERNMENT OF THE CITY OF CHESTER.

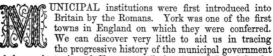 UNICIPAL institutions were first introduced into Britain by the Romans. York was one of the first towns in England on which they were conferred. We can discover very little to aid us in tracing the progressive history of the municipal government of the ancient city of Chester, until the time of Ranulph, the third Earl Palatine and nephew of the Earl Hugh ; but being

a Roman colony, the inhabitants no doubt were regarded as
Roman citizens, and as such entitled to the same privileges
which Rome itself possessed. Pennant supposes that the Roman prœtorium occupied the site on which St. Peter's church
is now built. In this tribunal, if the case be so, the civil law
and power would be exercised in those days.

Before the city had any charter, says King's 'Vale Royal,'
"they used by prescription divers liberties, and enjoyed a guild
mercatory, that is, a brotherhood of merchants, and that whatsoever was not admitted of that society, he could not use any
trade, or traffick within the city, nor be a tradesman therein.
And the tenor of this guild mercatory did even run in these
words : — Sicut hactenus usi fuerint ; and was after confirmed under the Earl's seal. And there was appointed two
overseers, and those were appointed out of the chiefest of
the citizens, and were greatly respected of the citizens as officers that had the special care of maintaining those privileges,
before a mayor was ordained."   These officers were elected
annually, and were denominated leave-lookers ; they were
accustomed to go round the city to see that its privileges
were preserved, and sometimes used to take small sums, called
leave-lookerage, for *leave* for non-freemen to sell wares by retail.

In the reign of Edward the Confessor, the government of
the city was vested in twelve judges, selected from the vassals
of the king, the earl, and the bishop.

The first charter granted to the city was by the first Ranulph,
also styled Ranulph le Meschin, third Earl of Chester, who
died in 1128. It grants to his tenants demesne of Chester,
that none but they or their heirs shall buy or sell merchandise,
brought to the city by sea or land, except at the fairs holden
at the nativity of St. John the Baptist, and on the feast of
St. Michael : and is directed thus—Ranul. com. Cestriæ. con-
stabulario. dupifero justiciar. vicecom. baron. militibus bullivis
et omnibus servientibus suis præsentibus et futuris, salutem ;
Sciatis, &c. ; and so makes a large grant to the city, and warrants
the same strongly against his heirs, and appoints forfeitures
upon all that shall withstand. The charter, which is without
date, is witnessed by Domino Hugone, Abbate Cestriæ. Domino
Hugone le Orebi, tunc. justiciar. Warren de Vernon, &c. &c.
It was confirmed by the other two Earls Ranulphs, and
also by Earl John, who strictly prohibited all buying and
selling except as aforesaid, with other additions.   King John
and Henry the Second also established it, with the addition
of some further privileges.   Henry the Third granted three
charters, in the first of which he recites, that he hath seen the
former charters of the earls, and doth grant and confirm domesticis

B 2

hominibus Cestr. &c., that none shall buy or sell merchandise
in the city, but citizens, except in the fairs, &c. subpœna £10.

It was at this time that, so far as we can ascertain, the first
mayor was created.* In the 26th year of Henry's reign, Sir
Walter Lynnet was the first who was invested with civic
honours and authority. The mayoralty of Chester is, therefore, a very ancient one, only 58 years younger we believe
than that of London.

In 1300 Edward the First confirmed the former charter of
his father, Henry the Third; and by the same charter gave
the city of Chester, with the appurtenances, liberties, and free-
doms to the citizens of Chester and their heirs, to be holden
of him and his heirs for ever, paying yearly £100. He granted
them also the election of coroners and pleas of the crown,
and that the citizens shall have sock, sack, toll, theme, infang-
theof, outfangtheof, and to be free throughout all the land
and dominion of toll, passage, &c.

Many other charters follow, and other matters connected
with the government of the city, which it is unnecessary to
recapitulate here.

Richard the Second in 1347, "for the furtherance of justice
and better execution thereof, grants unto his subjects, maiors,
sheriffs, and commonality of the said city, to hold their courts;
and limited what processes they may award in actions, personal
felonies, appeals, process of uttagary, as at the common law;"
and since then the sessions of the peace have continued to be
held down to the present time.

Henry Seventh, "In consideration that through the decay of
the haven and river, by many burstings forth, was become
sandy and impassable, as before, for merchandise," remitteth
£80 annually of the fee farm rent. And the said King Henry
Seventh granteth that the City of Chester and the suburbs,
towns, and hamlets thereof, the castle excepted, should be a
county of itself, by the name of the county of Chester.

Henry the Eighth sent letters in parchment under his privy
seal to the Mayor of Chester, charging that the citizens should
not be pressed unto the war, but remain within the city for
the defence thereof. He also, by letters patent, discharged
the city from being a sanctuary for malefactors, which was by
proclamation removed to Stafford. In the 32nd year of the
same reign, the city obtained the privilege of returning two
burgesses as its representatives in the English parliament.

The important changes effected in the muncipal corporations
of England and Wales in 1835, render it unnecessary to enter
further into the various charters granted to the city of Chester.

* Ormerod's Cheshire, page 173.

By that Act, the local government was vested in town council-lors, elected by the people at large, and who serve for a term of three years. Chester is divided into five wards for the election of the council; each ward elects six councillors, two of whom retire from office annually. The councillors elect ten aldermen, who hold their office for six years; and any member of the council is eligible to the office of mayor.

The following is a list of those who have served the office of mayor of Chester :—

1251	Sir Walter Lynnett, Knt.	1758	Thos. Grosvenor, Esq.
1677	William Ince, Esq.	1759	Thos. Cholmondeley, Esq.
1696	Peter Bennet, Esq.	1760	Thos. Cotgreave, Esq.
1700	Hugh Starkie, Esq.	1761	Holme Burrows, Esq.
1702	William Earl of Derby.	1763	Edward Burrows, Esq.
1704	Edward Partington, Esq.	1764	George French, Esq.
1705	Edward Puleston, Esq.	1765	Sir W. W. Wynn, Bart.
1708	James Mainwaring, Esq.	1769	Gabriel Smith, Esq.
1709	William Allen, Esq.	1773	Panton Ellamies, Esq
1710	Thomas Partington, Esq.	1779	Thomas Amery, Esq.
1711	John Minshull, Esq.	1781	Henry Higg, Esq.
1712	John Thomason, Esq.	1783	John Hallwood, Esq.
1714	Francis Sayer, Esq.	1784	William Harrison, Esq.
1715	Jno. Stringer, Esq.	1787	Sir Rd. Grosvenor, Bart.
1715	Sir Richd. Grosvenor, Brt.	1795	Richd. Ollerhead, Esq.
1716	Henry Bennett, Esq.	1803	Edmund Bushell, Esq.
1717	John Hodgson, Esq.	1807	Robt. Earl Grosvenor
1718	Alexander Denton, Esq.	1809	Thomas Evans, Esq.
1719	Randle Bingley, Esq.	1810	Thomas Grosvenor, Esq.
1720	Thomas Edwards, Esq.	1811	Robt. Bowers, Esq.
1725	John Parker, Esq.	1813	Sir W. W. Wynn, Bart.
1729	Thomas Brock, Esq.	1814	John Bedward, Esq.
1731	Trafford Massie, Esq.	1815	Sir J. Cotgreave, Knt.
1733	Peter Ellamies, Esq.	1816	Thos. Francis, Esq.
1734	Roger Massie, Esq.	1817	Henry Bowers, Esq.
1736	W. W. Wynn, Esq.	1818	Thos. Bradford, Esq.
1737	Sir Rbt. Grosvenor, Bart.	1819	John Williamson, Esq.
1738	Nathl. Wright, Esq.	1820	Wm. Seller, Esq.
1743	Thomas Davies, Esq.	1821	John S. Rogers, Esq.
1744	Thomas Maddock, Esq.	1822	Wm. Massey, Esq.
1745	Henry Ridley, Esq.	1823	Robt. Morris, Esq.
1746	Edward Yearsley, Esq.	1824	Geo. Harrison, Esq.
1747	William Edwards, Esq.	1825	John Fletcher, Esq.
1748	Edward Griffith, Esq.	1826	John Larden, Esq.
1750	John Hallwood, Esq.	1827	Thomas Francis, Esq.
1754	Wm. Cooper, Esq., M.D.	1827	Henry Bowers, Esq.
1757	Richd. Richardson, Esq.	1828	Robert Morris, Esq.

1829 William Moss, Esq.	1840 The same
1830 Titus Chaloner, Esq.	1841 Wm. Wardell, Esq.
1831 Richd. Buckley, Esq.	1842 Wm. Brown, Esq.
1831 Geo. Harrison, Esq.	1843 Wm. Hny. Brown, Esq.
1832 John Fletcher, Esq.	1844 Henry Kelsall, Esq.
1833 Geo. Harrison, Esq.	1845 Charles Potts, Esq.
1834 The same	1846 Edward Tilston, Esq.
1835 The same	1847 R. P. Jones, Esq., M.D.
1836 William Cross, Esq.	1848 The same
1837 Thos. Dixon, Esq.	1849 Sir E. S. Walker, Knt.
1838 Ed. Saml. Walker, Esq.	1850 John Williams, Esq.
1839 John Uniacke, Esq.	1851 The same

ROMAN ANTIQUITIES.

E have already intimated that Chester is very remarkable for the many antiquities which have been discovered here at various periods of its history; and as every vestige of this enterprizing and powerful people is possessed of intense interest and importance, because of the aid thus furnished in historic investigation;—for the sake of those who are in quest of such materials, and are prepared to appreciate their value, we will proceed to direct the attention of the reader to some of the relics for which Chester is famous, referring the antiquary to the works of Leycester, King, Pennant, Ormerod, and Hanshall, for a more minute description.

Altars, Roman pavements, pigs of lead, coins, and other precious relics of former times, have been discovered in various places in the city and neighbourhood, some of them within a very recent period. Now that the people are happily being taught to estimate local antiquities at their proper worth, and a spirit of inquiry is being invoked respecting them, it is to be hoped that any future discoveries that may be made, will be carefully preserved. There is no doubt that, through recklessness or ignorance, many links in the chain of our local history have been neglected and lost.

On a projecting rock in Handbridge, situate at the south end of the bridge, is a sculptured figure of Minerva, with her symbol, the owl. Time, with his silent tooth, has very much obliterated and defaced this ancient sculpture, called Edgar's cave, which is generally regarded by historians as of Roman date. Close to the figure is a great hole in the rock; and the field in which it is situated is known by the name of Edgar's field to the present day.

In the year 1653 an altar, supposed to have been dedicated to Jupiter, was dug up in Foregate-street, and which is preserved among the Arundelian marbles at Oxford. The back of it is plain : on the sides of it there are neatly sculptured a Patera, a

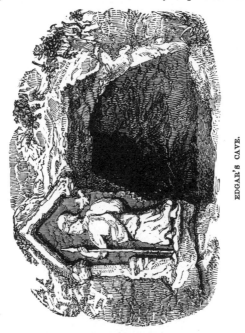

EDGAR'S CAVE.

cup which was used in their libations ; and a Thuribulum, or censer for burning incense. The inscription when perfect was—

I . O . M . TANARO
T . ELVPIVS . GALER
PRAESENS . GUNTA
PRI . LEG . XX . V . V
COMMODO . ET . LATERANO
COS
V . S . L . M

which Leigh, in his 'Natural History of Lancashire and Cheshire,' explains thus—

JOVI OPTIMO MAXIMO TANARO
TITUS ELUPIUS GALERIUS
PRÆSENS GUBERNATOR
PRINCIBUS LEGIONIS VICESSIMÆ VICTRICIS VALERIÆ
COMMODO ET LATERANO CONSULIBUS,
VOTUM SOLVIT LUBENS MERITO.

In the year 1693, on the occasion of digging a place for a cellar in Eastgate-street, an altar was found buried amongst a great quantity of ashes, horns, and bones of several animals. On the back of the altar is represented a curtain with a festoon, over which is a globe surrounded with palm branches. On one side is a vase with two handles, from which issue acanthus leaves, supporting a basket of fruit ; on the other side is a Genius with a Cornucopia in his left hand, and an altar on his right: on the top of the altar is a well sculptured human face within the Thuribulum.

This altar was found with the inscription downwards, and near it were two medals, one of Vespasian, the other is assigned to Constantius Chlorus, son-in-law of Maximian. The inscription, with restorations, runs thus :—

PRO . SAL . DOMIN

ORUM . NN . INVI

CTISSIMORVM

AVGG . GENIO . LOCI

FLAVIVS . LONGVS

TRIB . MIL . LEG . XX . VV

LONGINVS . FIL

EIVS . DOMO

SAMOSATA

V . S

Mr. Roach Smith says, "The persons who erected this altar were of Samosata, a town of Syria, celebrated as the birth-place of Lucian."

In 1779 an altar was found in Watergate-street, which is still preserved in the grounds of Oulton Park, the seat of Sir Philip de Malpas Grey Egerton, Bart., M.P. : at the sides are the rod of Esculapius, the Cornucopiæ and rudder, a patera, urn, sacrificial knife and other instruments. The inscription, with a few restorations, is as follows :—

FORTVNAE . REDVCI
ESCVLAP . ET . SALVTI . EIVS
LIBERT . ET . FAMILIA
CAII . PONTII . T . F . CAL . MAMILIANI
RVFI . ANTISTIANI . FVNINSVLANI
VETTONIANI . LEG . AVG
D . D

In the year 1821 a handsome altar was found by some
labourers in a field called "the Daniels," in Great Boughton,
near Chester, between the Tarvin and Huntingdon roads: it
is now preserved at Eaton Hall, the seat of the Marquis of
Westminster. It is of red sand stone : the mouldings are
bold, but it has no other ornaments upon it except the scrolls
which support the Thuribulum. The inscription is the same
on both sides, and is as follows :—

It has been supposed probable that the reason why this
altar was erected on that particular spot, was because of the
pure water that springs on that side of the town : the old

abbot's well is in that quarter, from which water was formerly conveyed by pipes to some of the monasteries in Chester.

Dr. Gale gives an inscription *(Antonini It.* p. 53) which he states to have been found at Chester : it is not known from whence it came :—

DEAE

NYMPHAE

BRIG

In 1729, in digging a cellar in Watergate-street, a stone was found with an inscription, of which the following fragment only remains :—

NVMINI . AVG

ALMAE . CET

NVS . ACTOR

EX . VOTO . FACI

In the Chapter-house of Chester Cathedral, there is a red sand stone, 24 inches by 8 inches, found on the site of the Deanery, bearing this inscription :—

COH . I . C . OCRATI

MAXIMINI . M . P

Mr. Roach Smith, an eminent authority in such matters, says that this inscription is to be ascribed to the century of Ocratius Maximus, of the first Cohort of the 20th Legion ; it has evidently been a facing stone, probably in the city wall; it resembles in character the centurial commemorations on the stones in the great northern wall, and like them, apparently refers to the completion of a certain quantity of building.

In the year 1738, in digging the foundation of a house in the market-place, a fragment of a slate stone was found, on which was cut in bas relief, the figure of a Retiarius armed with his trident and net, and a considerable part of the shield of the Secutor. The Secutores and the Retiarii were gladiators distinguished by their armour and manner of fighting.

They bore in their left hand a trident, and in the right a net, with which the combatant attempted to entangle his adversary, by throwing it over his head, and suddenly drawing it together, and then with his trident he usually slew him.

Horsley describes a small statue of stone found near the Dee, supposed to be either Atys or Mithras. It had a Phrygian bonnet, a mantle on the shoulders, a short vest on the body, and a declining torch in the hands.

On pulling down the old Eastgate in 1768, some portions of the original Roman structure were discovered, consisting of four arches, two in a line, and fifteen feet distant from each other; between the two arches fronting the east, was a statue of the god Mars, holding in his right hand a spear handle, and his left resting on a shield. This was cut in one large stone of about a half ton weight. There was also found a piece of rude sculpture about two feet in height, representing a Roman soldier.

In the year 1800 a Roman Ring, with an onyx stone in the centre, was found by some workmen when digging in a garden in Upper Northgate-street, and is now in the possession of R. J. Hastings, Esq. of this City.

In 1803 part of a mosaic pavement, about five feet square, was discovered about six feet below the surface of the earth, on digging a cellar in what was then known by the name of the Nuns' Garden, near the Castle.

In 1813, in sinking the foundation of a cellar at Netherleigh House, a short distance from Chester, a considerable number of large vases of red clay were discovered; they were regularly arranged in vaults, each vault containing four or six vases. Some of these were filled with calcined bones and small lumps of white clay. One of the vases was secured in a perfect state, but the others in most part were destroyed, through the carelessness of the workmen. A demi figure, habited in a sacerdotal costume, was found at the same time.

In 1814 a tesselated pavement was discovered near the gateway of the Castle, in making the alterations there, part of which was destroyed, and the remainder covered up again.

In April, 1850, whilst excavating for a drain on the premises belonging to Mr. Wynne, carpenter, on the east side of Bridge-street, adjoining the Feathers-lane, a portion of a tile flooring was discovered, in a remarkably good state of preservation, and which is supposed to be medieval. This floor was made the subject of an interesting lecture by Mr. Harrison, architect, which is embodied in the valuable report published by the Chester Archæological Society. Large square Roman tiles of red clay are frequently found in removing old buildings, and

breaking up the pavements in Chester. Many of these are
stamped with the inscription of the 20th Legion, LEG. XX.
VV. and others are marked LEG. VV. Œ.

These tiles were manufactured by the soldiers of the Legion,
who, we find from history, were accomplished masons, being
trained to use the pick-axe, spade, and trowel, as well as
military arms. In times of peace they were employed in
building houses and public edifices, constructing roads, and
tilling the fields. To them "we are indebted for nearly all
the inscriptions discovered in this country, which abound in
the districts where they were regularly quartered, or employed
on public works, and are comparatively scarce in other localities."

A great number of coins have been found at various times
within the walls of Chester, of Vespasian, Trajan, Hadrian, Fl.
Val. Constantius, and other Roman emperors, some in brass and
others in silver. A very fine gold coin of Faustina the elder, wife
of Antonius Pius, was found a few years ago near the castle; and
in 1826 a very beautiful gold coin was dug up in a field at the
east end of Capt. Wrench's house, which is in the possession of
Captain Wrench. On the obverse is the head of Nero, with
his title NERO CÆSAR AVGVSTVS, and on the reverse is a figure
in a sitting posture, and the legend SALVS.

Whilst excavating a drain in Grosvenor-street, in 1828,
several coins were found, some of which were in very good
preservation, especially one of Trajan and another of Geta.
A lamp made of lead, and an ivory stylus were also dug up
at the same time. In the same year was found near the
new church of St. Bridget, a small altar, without any inscription to assist the antiquarian in ascertaining anything respecting its dedication. Within the space of a few inches from the
altar was found a brass medal, on which the figure of the god
Neptune is clearly delineated, with his trident, and a ship
with her sails. The legend on it is NEPTVNVS ; on the reverse
is Hercules with his club, and a female figure by his side,
and around is the inscription HERCVLES ET PALLAS.

A short time ago a small votive altar was found by W. Ayrton,
Esq. at Boughton, near to the spot where the altar, dedicated

to the Nymphs, was discovered, which we have already described. We have exhibited it in the annexed engraving. The inscription has been interpreted thus :—

GENO. AVERNI. IVL. QVNTILIANVS.

Julius Quintilianus to the genius of Avernus.

Examples of dedication to genii are very numerous; the belief that they presided over the welfare of cities, families, and individuals, was part of the religious system of the Romans. It was generally believed that every individual had two genii, the one good, the other bad. With reference to the particular inscription to the genius Avernus, Mr. Roach Smith says, "that he finds no other mention : but the locality in which the altar was found, confirms the literal interpretation that the genius of the well known lake in Carpania is here to be understood as addressed by Julius Quintilianus. The waters of the lake were much used by the Romans in magical rites, as the classical reader will be reminded by the line in Virgil's description of the incantation scene, preparatory to Dido's death :—

Sparserat et latices simulatos fontis Averni.

A short time ago there was found in Common Hall Street, embedded in a thick wall several feet under ground, a block or pig of lead, which we exhibit in the annexed cut:—

Unfortunately the inscription has only been partially preserved, inasmuch as it presents a different reading from others which have been discovered, and which Camden mentions as being very general in Cheshire; but those which he records as having come under his notice had inscribed on them—

IMP . DOMIT . AVG . GER . DE . CEANG.

These pigs of lead appear to have been paid as tribute by the Britons to their Roman masters, "the harsh exaction of which was one of the causes of the insurrection."

A great quantity of the Red Samian, and other kinds of pottery, have been discovered within the walls of Chester, which are supposed to have been of foreign origin. The names of the potters were:—

HIVNV.— SEV. . . .—BELINOIM.—ALBINVS.— BITVRIX.—ATILLVS.— VARIVS . F.— I | OFFIC.—CRESI . M.—PVONI . M.—E ᘏ CV ᘏ I . M.

The following recent discoveries we extract from the first report of the Chester Architectural, Archæological, and Historic Society, incorporated in a most able and interesting paper by C. Roach Smith, Esq.

Weaver-street.—In excavating for sewers, was found, at the depth of seven feet, a raised foot-path, edged with curb-stones, and a regular paved road, of marble stones, set in sand; four feet above this, a layer of charcoal; at ten or eleven feet deep, a quantity of Roman tile.

Commonhall-street.—Up the centre, a row of foundations formed of concrete (broken marble-stones in hard mortar), about nine feet apart, all in a line, and about ten feet deep, presenting the appearance of having supported columns. A large square block of stone, four feet two inches square, and sixteen inches deep, without lewis holes, on a bed of concrete. A portion of a column of very debased classical form, about two feet in diameter; at the top is a hole, four inches and a half square, and the same deep, and a similar hole at the bottom; the square part seems never to have been smoothly dressed; the workman said it was fast to the grouted concrete, at the depth of ten feet; mouldings, broken tiles, and pottery, coins of Pius, Tetricus, &c.; a quantity of animals' bones, a stag's skull, with the horns sawn off, and a wild boar's tusk. In the adjoining street, a moulded block of cornice, eight inches thick, on the under side of which is a rude inscription; embedded in a thick wall, at the same place, a pig of lead; a capital of a pillar. The tiles are of various forms, some overlapping one another; some with a kind of pattern or letters; others with marks of animals' feet. One, perfect, twenty-one inches by thirteen, of singular form. Also, what appears to have been a portion of a gable end."

In December, 1850, whilst fresh drains were being made, an old Roman Vase was found in a yard belonging to Mr. Parkinson, plumber, in Northgate Street, between the Abbey Square, and the Abbey Green. The labourer who was employed in the drain in that neighbourhood, unhappily shattered this vase in pieces. The fragments, however, were collected together with great care, and re-united by Mr. Parkinson, in whose possession it now remains. "There were found with it some portions of annular brass money, much corroded."

Near to the Feathers Hotel, in Bridge Street, in a cellar now occupied as an earthenware shop, are the remains of the Roman Hypocaust and sweating bath, the use of which appears to have been very general amongst the Romans, and regarded by them as one of their chief luxuries. From the details which have been handed down to us by ancient historians, respecting these curious erections, we learn that they were not only constructed so as to secure the comfort and convenience of the bathers to the fullest extent, but were often built in the most magnificent style of architecture. The one in Bridge Street, which circumstances have happily spared, is in a tolerably perfect state.*

It is fifteen feet long, and eight wide, and six feet seven inches deep. There is an adjoining chamber, or *præfurnium*, of the same dimensions. The Hypocaust is supported by twenty-eight square pillars, two feet eight inches high, and one foot square at the top and bottom. Over these pillars are placed bricks, eighteen inches square, and three inches thick, which support others two feet square, perforated with small holes, about six inches asunder, for the purpose of conveying the heat upwards. Immediately above this uppermost layer of bricks is a terrace floor, composed of several layers of lime, pounded bricks, &c.,

* A beautiful engraving of this bath has just been brought out by the publisher of this work, from a drawing by G. Pickering, Esq.

in different proportions and degrees of fineness. The room above is the Sudatorium or Sweating Room, which received the hot air from the Hypocaust below. Around the walls were benches, rising one above another, on which the bathers sat, until they burst out into a free perspiration; after which they were scraped with a bronze instrument called a *Strigil*— thin and flexible like a hoop, by which all impurities were removed from the skin; they were then *shampooed*, rubbed down with towels *(Lintea)*, and their bodies anointed with oil, by an attendant called *Aliptes*, after which they returned to the *Tepidarium*, where they attired themselves, and cooled gradually before returning to the open air.

In 1779, another Hypocaust, and the remains of several adjoining rooms of a Roman house, were discovered in digging the foundations of houses near the Watergate. The Hypocaust consisted of the same number of pillars as those which are to be seen near the Feathers Inn.

The Sudatory stood lower down, much nearer the gate: the upper floor was supported by twenty-four pillars composed of tiles, nine inches square and two inches thick, filled up with a fine red clay. On the top of each pillar was placed a tile two feet square, which seemed to have supported a double floor of coarse cement: round the sides of the room there appeared to have been a row of funnel bricks, fixed with their upper ends level with the surface of the floor, each tunnel having two opposite mortice holes for a cross passage to convey the heat more regularly over the sweating room. It was paved in a circular mosaic figure: the *tesserae* of which it was composed were of three different colours, viz., a dusky blue, a brick coloured red, and a yellowish white, of cubes not exceeding half an inch.

The pillars of this Hypocaust, the altar dedicated to *Fortuna Redux, Esculapius et Salus*, and a few other antiquities were found at the same time, and were removed to Oulton Park.

But small portions of the original Roman wall of Chester, we believe, now exist; the present wall, no doubt, stands on the same foundation. The Roman pavement has been often discovered at the depth of a few feet below the modern one, in the principal streets which, in all probability, run in the same direction as those of the Roman City.

In closing this brief enumeration of the Antiquities of Chester, we have only to express our earnest hope that a local museum may soon be established, especially devoted to the careful preservation of relics having reference to the county, perfectly classified and arranged, so that nothing may be lost which may serve to enlighten us on the history of the past.

A WALK ROUND THE WALLS OF CHESTER.

THE Chester walls are the only perfect specimen of this order of ancient fortification now to be met with in the kingdom. There is nothing, perhaps, which impresses a stranger more forcibly, or sooner attracts his interest and curiosity, than these embattled memorials of the olden times. The moment he beholds them, he is reminded of a state of things, which, happily, for centuries has ceased to exist. A comparison of the use to which they are now appropriated, with that to which they were devoted in days gone by, strikingly shews the genial change which has passed over the spirit of the people ; and the contrast may serve to render us more satisfied with the present age.

In "King's Vale Royal" it is stated that they were first built by Marius King of the Britons, A. D. 73. Leland and Selden, both authors of credit, attribute to the Romans the foundation of Chester. According to Geoffry of Monmouth, Higden, Bradshaw the Monk, and Stowe, it is of an origin more ancient than Rome itself, and was only re-edified by the legionaries; but, in support of their assertions, the aforesaid writers, all of whom delight in the marvellous, give no other authority save vague tradition. On the other hand, the Walls of Chester, at this hour, bear witness to the truth of Leland and Selden's account of their origin. In choosing the ground for their camps, the Romans usually fixed upon stations commanding an extensive view of the adjacent country, a constant supply of water, and (if possible) a communication with the sea. All these were to be found in Chester : and when it is added that the Walls still retain the exact form of the *agger* of the *castra hiberna* of the Romans,—that the Old Eastgate, which was evidently a *porta principalis*, stood in the line of the *Watling Way*,—and that there is evidence of the *prœtorium* having stood on the spot now occupied by St. Peter's Church, there is fair ground of belief that the Walls were originally the work of the Romans.

They are built of soft freestone, and command an extensive and beautiful prospect over many miles round. The view from the Northgate, with the Welsh Hills in the distance, is universally admired. The Walls are a mile and three quarters and one hundred and twenty-one yards in circumference, and are kept in repair by the Corporation.

We commence our perambulation at a flight of steps on the North side of the Eastgate. Proceeding to the right a short

distance, and the venerable Cathedral arrests our attention, seen in one of its best points of view, of which a lengthened description will be given as we proceed.

At the end of Abbey Street, is a small archway or passage through the Walls, leading to the Kale-yards or cabbage gardens, which formerly belonged to the Abbot and Convent of St. Werburgh. This opening was permitted to be made for their convenience in the reign of Edward I. to prevent the necessity of bringing their vegetables a circuitous round through the Eastgate.

A few paces farther on was a quadrangular abutment, on which formerly stood a tower called *The Sadler's Tower*, from the Company of Sadlers holding their meetings there. The tower was taken down in 1780; and the abutment, which marked the place where it stood, was taken down in 1828.

The elevated tower on the Canal bank belongs to the extensive Shot and White Lead Manufactory of Messrs. Walker, Parker, and Co., and forms a prominent object in the different approaches to the City.

The lofty tower which stands at the angle is called the

THE PHŒNIX TOWER,

which possesses intense interest, from the memorable incidents with which history identifies it. There are but few of these time-stricken towers remaining to perpetuate the hostile æra in which they were erected.

The Phœnix Tower was formerly used by some of the companies of the city, whose arms were placed upon it, as a chamber for business. Of these the *Phœnix*, the crest of the Painters' and Stationers' Company, which was put up in 1613, now only remains.

From the summit of this tower, King Charles I. had the mortification to see his army, under the generalship of Sir Marmaduke Langdale, defeated by the parliamentary forces, under their leader, General Pointz, at the battle of Rowton Moor, on the 27th September, 1645. From its elevation and command of view over the township of Newton, it was formerly called *Newton's Tower*. Linked as it is with that eventful battle during one of the most significant epochs of our national history, it is not surprising that it is always regarded with intense curiosity, as a suggestive memorial of most interesting occurrences. The mind is involuntarily carried back to the period when our country was involved in the discord, strife, and bloodshed of civil war; and, perhaps, as involuntarily reflects on the genial and happy change which the progress of knowledge, freedom, and religion, has accomplished in the minds and institutions of the people. We can now occupy the very spot on which the hapless monarch beheld the discomfiture of his hopes and power; but can now gaze upon a prospect very different to that which greeted his vision, and with emotions more grateful than those which then distracted the monarch's breast. His Majesty remained that night in Chester, and on the following day marched with 500 horse into Wales.

Beneath the Walls here, deeply cut in the solid rock, is the Ellesmere and Chester Canal.

Between the Eastgate and Phœnix Tower the remains of the Roman Walls are conspicuous in the lower courses. At the distance of about seven feet from the top of the parapet, the Roman portion is terminated by a cornice, which extends in broken lengths for at least 100 yards.

We may just state that, in the time of the great civil war, a ditch surrounded the Walls, from the Eastgate to the Water Tower. The view which is obtained from the elevation of this part of the Walls is very expansive and beautiful. As you approach the North from the Eastgate, the ranges of Peckforton Hills, Beeston Castle, and the Forest of Delamere, form the back ground of the landscape, marked on the foreground with Waverton and Christleton church; and still nearer the extensive Railway Station. This view embraces a rural district of more than a dozen miles in length.

Next we arrive at

THE NORTHGATE.

The ancient gate, over which the gaol was situated, and where criminals were formerly executed, was taken down in 1808, and the prisoners removed to a more commodious building on the south side of the infirmary.

The present gate is a handsome Doric structure, forming a capacious elliptic arch of white stone, divided from two smaller ones at the sides by two pillars. It was erected at the expense of the late Marquis of Westminster. The North side bears this inscription:

PORTAM SEPTENTRIONALEM SVBSTRVCTAM
A ROMANIS VETVSTATE JAM˜ DILAPSAM
IMPENSIS SVIS AB INTEGRO RESTITVENDAM
CVRAVIT ROBERTVS COMES GROSVENOR.
A. R. GEORGII TERTII LI.

On the South side is the following :—

INCHOTA GVLIELMO NEWELL ARM. MAI.
MDCCCVIII.
PERFECTA THOMA GROSVENOR ARM. MAI.
MDCCCX.
THOMA HARRISON ARCHITECTO.

The summit of this gate commands a most extensive and delightful prospect. On each side of the gate is a commodious flight of steps, by which the passenger may descend into Northgate Street.

Before the gate, and on the left hand of Upper Northgate-Street, stands the Blue-coat Hospital, which was founded by subscription in 1700, at the suggestion of Bishop Stratford; the greater part of the present structure was built in 1717, partly at the expense of the Corporation and partly by benefactions. Twenty-eight boys are boarded, clothed, and educated, from the age of 12 to 14. There are also sixty-four probationary day scholars, who succeed to the vacancies of the former. They are well educated in the various branches of useful knowledge, and at the age of 14 are provided with respectable situations.

The chapel, dedicated to St. John the Baptist, called Little St. John's, occupies the south wing of this building: it was formerly an hospital, or sanctuary, and endowed with great privileges. It is extra-parochial, and a perpetual curacy is in the gift of the corporation. The Rev. William Clarke is the present curate. The hospital is of great antiquity, having been founded by Randal Earl of Chester, for a master, three chaplains, and thirteen citizens of Chester, being either "poor or sillie, or poor or feeble persons." The mastership was granted in the ninth year of Edward Second, to the prior of Birkenhead.

The chapel and hospital being destroyed during the civil wars, were re-built by Col. Roger Whitley, to whom King Charles Second granted the hospital estate for his life and twenty years after. When the city charter was renewed in 1686, the reversions were granted to the mayor and citizens for ever, as trustees for the Hospital. The corporation obtained possession in 1703, and have since exercised the right of presentation; in the time of King Henry VIII. it consisted of a Chaplain and six poor brethren; and had lands and profits to the amount of twenty-eight pounds ten shillings and four-pence. There are now in the Chapel-yard six alms-houses for widows, who are each allowed £1 6s. 8d. a year and some perquisites. In 1801, Alderman Crewe bequeathed £30 per annum to be divided amongst them in equal proportions.

Proceeding on our circuit, we are next brought to a curious square building called MORGAN'S MOUNT, a platform on the right, accessible by a flight of steps, underneath which is a sort of chamber, apparently one of the stations for a sentinel. From the summit we have a wide-spreading and enchanting prospect, which is seldom surpassed; exhibiting the windings of the Dee to its estuary; Flint Castle; the Jubilee Column, on Moel

Fammau; the Light House, at the Point of Ayr; the beautiful
range of the Clwyddian hills; and the church and castle of
Hawarden.　On the right, a very excellent view is presented
of the

TRAINING COLLEGE,

which was erected from a design and under the superintendence
of Messrs. J. C. and G. Buckler, of London, at an estimated
cost of £10,000, raised by public subscription, assisted by a
grant from government, and was completed in September, 1842.
The institution is under the presidency of the Lord Bishop of
the diocese; and has the sanction of the Very Rev. The Deans
and the Rev. The Chapters of Chester and Manchester.　The
object it seeks to promote is, the supply of the parochial schools
of the Diocese of Chester with masters well qualified by a
sound, religious, and scientific training, for the discharge of their
important duties.　Hitherto, it has nobly sustained its purpose,
and by regularly sending forth men, whose minds have been
brought under thorough discipline, and well furnished with general knowledge and science, is doing very much towards the elevation of parochial education in the county.　The college is
under the able direction of the Rev. Arthur Rigg, M.A., of
Christ's College, Cambridge; the vice-principal is the Rev. W.
J. Constable, M.A., graduate of the same University.　A very
graphic and truthful description of the management and inward
operations of this important institution, written by an Irish
gentleman, appeared a short time ago in the ' Chester Courant,'
whose letter we will here insert :—

Royal Hotel, Chester, Sept. 1850.

" MY DEAR T.—I promised to send you a report of our
visit to the Training College; and for once you must be con-
tent with having a letter occupied with a single object, instead
of including, as a tourist's letter may naturally be expected to
do, the record of a variety of scenes over which his eye has
wandered.　Accompanied by your friend, who offered to introduce us, we drove to the College this morning, soon after
breakfast, and were delighted at once with the situation, and
the view which it commands.　The College stands on a rising
ground, just out of the town, on the road leading to Parkgate;
and the valley, through which the River Dee pursues its course
to the sea, rich in verdure and foliage, spreads before you;
bounded by the noble range of hills, I might almost say mountains, which separate the Vale of Clwyd from that of the Dee,
and form the north eastern frontier of the Principality.　Not to
dwell, however, on externals, we entered the building at the

western end, which, it seems, forms the residence of the Principal, and enquired for him. We were told that twelve o'clock
had struck, and that he had just left the class-room, and that
he was probably somewhere among the workshops. It seemed
odd to hear of workshops in a College ; but your friend who
knew all the ways of the house, desired us to follow him ; and
having passed through a small piece of kitchen garden, where
two young men in square caps, such as are worn in Cambridge,
were digging very neatly some borders into which plants were
to be set ; we went up a passage through which we entered a
yard, in one corner of which was a blacksmith's forge in full
activity. The bellows were working merrily ; quick and heavy
blows were falling on a piece of red hot iron ; and bright sparks
were flying in every direction from the anvil ; while two men
were striking, and half a dozen lads were busy, either in working the bellows or in subjecting pieces of metal to the fire.
"Mr. Principal," said your friend, "I have brought you some
visitors, who wish to see the College, but do not let us disturb
you, if you are busy." One of the workmen stopped, and
briefly saying that he was quite at our service, he threw off
the leather apron which he had been wearing, put the sledge-
hammer into the hands of a stout youth who had been standing by, told him in a word how he was to go on, and then
presented himself to us as the Rev. Arthur Rigg, late of Christ
College, Cambridge, and Principal of the College at Chester.
I could not but ask him what he was about ; as I certainly
wished to know what it was that had turned a learned eccle-
siastic into a blacksmith, and whether it was fancy or amusement that led to this unusual employment. He told me
with great good nature, that they were employed in making
turning lathes for sale, and that they forged the bar iron into
the pieces from which the screws and other parts of the machine were made ; and that he had merely taken the hammer
in order to show the others the way in which the iron was to
be welded. He pointed to a number of tools, such as chisels,
&c., which were hanging upon the walls, and said, "we make
all these things here ; and you will soon see how many we
need and the use to which we turn them." My ladies looked
half frightened at this vestibule into which their wish to see the
College had carried them ; but Mr. R. began to talk to them at
once as he led the way out of the yard ; and I was entertained
by seeing how much and how rapidly he laid hold of their attention. "It is our playtime," he said, "the men have just left
their studies, and we shall find them scattered about the premises, doing what they like in the way of amusement till dinner
time ; and the ladies will be more entertained by seeing their

recreations than they could be by seeing them absorbed in cal-
culations in the class-room, or bothered with books.   Down
these steps, he added, and we shall find them all at work."
We followed him down a short flight of steps, which led into
a large subterraneous room, like a well-lighted cellar; and it
seemed as if we had got into the workshop of the world.
Fifteen or twenty young men, with rather a larger number of
boys, were all at work: but all so busy, so merry, and so
deeply interested in what they were about, that they took no
notice of us, and went on hammering, sawing, turning, and
grinding, as if their livelihood depended on what they did.
Gradually as I recovered my senses and was able to look round,
I found one group occupied with a lithographic press, striking
off circulars from stone. I found a long table surrounded by
others who were executing with extraordinary correctness some
Gothic mouldings in oak. A circular saw, which was set in
motion by a large wheel, was cutting deal plank into slips
with as much rapidity as if it had been paper; and in the
further end there were several turning lathes at work, and
articles of use were being thrown off in quick succession.
Half a dozen other crafts were, I believe, going on in other
corners, and in a laboratory near the door I found three little
fellows occupied in colouring glass, and two others were finishing some excellent models of the steam-engine and power-loom.
The scene was in truth most extraordinary : and I must own
the universal animation and goodness which pervaded the
party was as wonderful as their activity. All seemed at work,
but without collision ; the boys seemed to have their own
departments as well as the men, and not one stepped beyond
his line, nor did more than he was wished to do, or able to do.
We must not stay here too long, said Mr. R. as he saw the
ladies watching with interest the working off of the copies of
the lithographic press; there are some other things that you
should see, and the time is short. We followed him to another
workshop, where the boys were making those card board models
for linear drawing, which you have seen in use at ———, and
which are now recommended by the best masters. They were
working on geometrical rules, and were evidently doing their
work both accurately and neatly, and two others were hard at
work binding a book. In an adjoining room there were half a
dozen more employed in a chemical experiment; in the laboratory two others were melting some brass ornaments out of
which they were to construct a paper weight; and in the
midst of them, a tall gentleman-like person, with something
more of an academical look than the Rev. Principal, was preparing for a lecture on Agricultural Chemistry by mixing in

separate saucers the earths of which he was to give an analysis in the evening.   We were introduced to him as the Vice-Principal, and he explained briefly the nature of the lecture for which he was arranging the materials, and in which his young companions seemed to take considerable interest by the attention they paid to what he said.

Passing through these rooms, we followed the Principal into another workshop, where a small steam-engine of singularly neat construction, was in full operation.   It was moving six or eight lathes, and iron and brass were being turned into screws, or holes were being drilled through plates of the same metal, with a rapidity which astonished us; and our astonishment was no doubt increased, when I heard from the friend who introduced and accompanied us, that the steam engine had been constructed by the students in their leisure hours, and that the whole apparatus which I saw was literally home-made, from the engine itself down to the tools with which the men were working.

The ladies, however, were now growing weary, and Mr. R. kindly proposed that they should go into his house to take some refreshment; but they wished to proceed, and we did proceed.   We passed, however, through his house, and were introduced to his lady, who kindly insisted on accompanying us through the interior.   Under her escort we went on, and saw the two large class-rooms, and admired the excellent system of ventilation, which secured to each a continued influx of warm but pure air; and then on the two upper stories of the house, we saw the dormitories of the men who are training as masters for schools; and that for the boys in the commercial school, which is above.   In these dormitories each individual has his separate cell, a cell just large enough to hold an iron bedstead, a wash-hand stand, and chest of drawers; all lighted up by gas at the hour of retiring, and all lights extinguished at the same minute.   We saw the separate apartment called the hospital, which, happily, has hardly ever been used, but which contains a good sitting-room, together with four sleeping rooms, differing only from the others in this, that each room is on a larger scale, and has a small fireplace.   We descended to the kitchen, a lofty, light, and spacious room, where an excellent dinner for about 90 hungry men and boys was being cooked by a fire which was less than that which I frequently see in your drawing-room; and we also saw the tables prepared in the hall, for the reception of the whole body.   Beyond the hall, we proceeded by a short passage to the College chapel; and here alone can anything like ornament be traced.   Throughout, the building is as simple as it possibly can be, though the mass is imposing, and the outline forms a group of no ordinary beauty. The chapel, however, is elegant. It was elegant in its original design ; but the interior is now receiving continued increase of embellishment, through the labour of the young men, who are filling up the pannels with mouldings on the best and purest form, and who beyond this are endeavouring to purchase the embellishment of painted windows by the sale of works done in their hours of recreation. When that decoration shall be added, few mansions of our nobility, few Colleges in either University will possess a building so chaste in design, and so appropriate in its style as the one of which I am writing.

While we were occupied in admiring this very striking scene, the dinner bell had summoned the men and boys from their workshops, and after a very hasty toilette, had collected them in the class-room. We heard the hymn chanted, which is used before meals, and as they slowly filed through the rooms and took their places at the table, the harmony of sound was sustained. The music indeed then ceased, and the clatter of knives and forks testified to the appetite with which the meal was welcomed, after the exertions, bodily as well as mental, included in the morning's employments. My companions were loud in expressing their admiration of what they had seen; but I own that on my mind there was another feeling still more predominant. I had long been thinking and enquiring on the subject of education. I had long been wishing to find a place where a really useful and practical education might be got. I had considered the plans of Pestalozzi, of Fellenberg ; and I had been prepared to run some risk and much expense, in order to obtain what I wanted, and here, to my surprise, I seemed to find it, combined with the strictest moral discipline, and the soundest religious training, and offered at a price infinitely lower than I had been prepared to expect. The charge was stated as being £30 for a boy below twelve years, and £35 for a boy above, without any of the various *et ceteras* which swell out the accounts at schools of a different description.

When at last it was necessary to take leave, I turned to the Principal, and whilst expressing my grateful acknowledgment of his courtesy, and for the pleasure he had given us, I could not help intimating my surprise that I had previously heard so little of a place of which so much might be said. He smiled and said—"Perhaps, sir, it is owing to our motto, for our motto intimates the principle on which we act here." He said this and pointed to a scroll which is placed over a large book-case at the end of the class-room. I looked up and read—"Without noise, without bustle, and without fame." Such has been the employment of the morning. I have written this description,

while the objects were fresh in my memory; and now let me
hear what you think of Mr. Principal, and of his principle.

Yours truly,
"E. T."

P.S.—If you should think of sending your nephew here, let me
tell you that the boys in the commercial school are mixed with
the young men who are being educated as schoolmasters only
at the hours of play and at their meals. The studies are conducted separately and in different rooms. The boys in the
commercial school learn all that is taught at common schools,
such as arithmetic, geography, English grammar, and learn it
fully and thoroughly. They may also learn Latin, French,
and German, if their parents choose; and they are all grounded
in the theory of music and linear drawing. I own, however,
that the knowledge they may gain in the workshops is, in my
opinion, more valuable than any other; for I know no other
place where it can be gained; and I see the purposes of use-
fulness to which it may be turned. Nor can I forget that
this knowledge, which may be so useful, is being gained while
other boys are only learning how to play at cricket, or wast-
ing their time in idleness and mischief."*

A few paces further on is an ancient tower, formerly called
Goblin's Tower, but now known by the name of PEMBERTON'S
PARLOUR. Being in a ruinous condition, part of it was taken
down in 1702, and the remainder renovated and repaired. On
the front was some excellent carved work in stone, and the
names of the Mayor (the Earl of Derby) and the other corporate
officers of the year in which the repairs were made; but in
consequence of the stone being of a soft and friable nature,
and from other causes, both the inscription and the carved
work are now almost obliterated. The inscription, so far as
it is legible, is as follows:—

* In the Minutes of the Committee of Council on Education for 1850,
there are the following remarks by the Rev. Henry Moseley, upon the
Chester Training College:—

"I have to bear the same testimony as heretofore to the excellent discipline of the Institution; to the great order that pervades it; and to the
judicious arrangements made in respect to the industrial training of the
Students: the industry, cheerfulness and activity, with which these
labours are pursued, in the intervals of study, is most pleasing to con-
templato. I know no other Training School, which, in respect to these
things, appears to me superior to this; and I attach to them, in a moral
point of view, the first importance. Nor do I know any other in which
the buildings appear to me better adapted to the use of a Training School,
or in which those minor arrangements, on which the domestic comfort of
the inmates and the good order of the household depend, are more carefully observed."

" * * * year of the glorious reign of Queen Anne, divers wide breaches in these walls were re-built, and other decays therein were repaired ; 2000 yards of the pavement were new flagged or paved, and the whole repaired, regulated, and adorned at the expense of £1000 and upwards. Thomas Hand, Esq., Mayor, 1701. The Right Honourable William, Earl of Derby, Mayor, 1702, who died in his Mayoralty." On the left is a large field, anciently called *Barrow Field*, which was used by the Roman soldiers for their military exercises ; a vast number of bodies were buried here at one of the periods when the plague raged so severely in the City.

Continuing our route westward, we next come to

THE WATER TOWER,

which is evidently an ancient fortress, erected for the purpose of repelling the approach of maritime foes, for it appears that formerly the river flowed under this part of the walls, so that vessels could sail close by the Tower. At high tide, the whole of the land on which are now situated Crane-street and the neighbourhood, was covered with water. At the south angle of the walls is an old square tower, anciently called *Bonwaldesthorne's Tower*, from which is an embattled passage to the Water Tower, which was built in 1322, by contract for £100, by John Helpstone, a mason. The dimensions were 24 yards in height and $10\frac{1}{3}$ yards in diameter. It had openings for cannon and rings in the walls to which ships were formerly moored. This noble bulwark is suggestive of reflections of deep historic interest ; for at the seige of Chester by the republican army, this place was bombarded from the farm-house called Brewer's Hall, on the opposide side of the river, but without success. Many a gallant sentinel has here kept loyal watch against the approach of the enemy. Happily, our age needs not these ancient fortifications for the warlike purpose to which they were originally devoted, and as an exhibition of the genius of the 13th and 19th centuries in happy contrast, this Tower, built for war, is now occupied as a

MUSEUM OF THE MECHANICS' INSTITUTION,

and is devoted to the more beneficent object of science and general improvement. Although the Museum is but of recent origin, the zeal and liberality of its supporters have already well furnished it with valuable relics, which will interest the antiquary and other curiosities of more modern date, which afford gratification to all. The munificent liberality of William Wardell, Esq., a devoted friend to every enterprise which contemplates the social and intellectual advancement of the citizens, enables us to point out a most attractive object in the

CAMERA OBSCURA,

which is situated on the upper part of the tower, and is well worthy of notice. We can promise the reader very great gratification and amusement from this excellent instrument, which will furnish him with a most charming prospect of the diversified and lovely scenery which nature has here so profusely spread around. The beautiful view of the winding Dee and the picturesque country on its banks is most delightful, and cannot fail to excite very pleasurable emotions. On the top of the tower is fixed a very good telescope by Dolland, which enables us to command a most extensive and magnificent view. If the day be favourable, and the atmosphere clear, we can stretch our gaze over a wide and truly grand range of objects, embracing the Great Ormshead at Llandudno, in Carnarvonshire, The Wrekin, in Shropshire, Moel Fammau and the Welsh Hills towering aloft in their imposing majesty. Across the river is Brewer's Hall, which we have mentioned, where Cromwell's army erected a battery, for the purpose of destroying this tower, "but which had no great effect;" close by is the Railway Viaduct of 47 arches, and the Bridge crossing the Dee on cast-iron girders; the whole scene forming an exceedingly fine panorama.

At the foot of the flight of steps close by are the City Baths and Wash-houses. The swimming bath is very capacious, and the necessary adjuncts most complete; there is also a fine shower bath, both being made tepid in spring, autumn, and winter.

We now resume our walk; and proceeding southwards from the Water Tower, on the left, in a beautiful and salubrious situation, is

THE INFIRMARY;

A handsome brick building, founded by Dr. William Stratford, who bequeathed £300 to the charity. It was opened on the 17th March, 1761. It is capable of containing 100 beds, with commodious offices, and excellent accommodation for its respective officers. The north part of the building is exclusively devoted to a fever ward. This asylum for the afflicted is liberally supported by voluntary subscriptions, and in its medical and domestic management, perhaps second to none in the kingdom. There are hot, cold, and vapour baths in the house, for the benefit of the patients; new baths have also been recently opened for the accommodation of the public. Donors of twenty guineas, and subscribers of two guineas per annum, are governors, with the privilege of recommending two in-patients, and six out-door patients annually.

The inmates receive the most humane and skilful attention from the medical staff, which consists of Llewellyn Jones, Esq. M.D.; R. P. Jones, Esq. M.D.; J. Edwards, Esq. M.D.; John Harrison, Esq.; T. Brittain, Esq.; J. Weaver, Esq.; Consulting Surgeon, G. Harrison, Esq.; House and Visiting Surgeon, William S. Jones, Esq.; Assistant, A. L. Slater, Esq.

The number of patients admitted during the year 1849 were,

In-patients	797
Home-patients	1621
Out-patients	1881

The total number since the foundation of the institution, 201,891.

Of all the charitable institutions which do honour to the benevolence of the city, the Infirmary ranks the first in beneficial and important operations, and eminently merits the sympathy and support of the public.

The next large building close by is

THE CITY GAOL,

which also includes the HOUSE OF CORRECTION; both are under the superintendence of a committee of the Town Council. The Gaol is in the western part of the building, with a handsome Doric entrance. Over the front entrance, within the iron railing, the condemned criminals are executed; which revolting spectacle, we are happy to say, has but very seldom to be witnessed. The entrance to the House of Correction is at the east end, and is also of stone. Each of these establishments has four courts with cells and day rooms adjoining; and both are under the government of one gaoler, and a male and female assistant. There is a chapel common to both establishments. The chaplain is appointed by the Corporation. In consequence of the escapes the prisoners have succeeded in making from time to time, many improvements have been made in the internal arrangements of the prison, since it was first built, respecting the classification of prisoners and other matters; and the outworks of the building have received some important additions to ensure their greater security. A little further on to the left is Stanley Place, a pleasant open square , of elegant, modern residences; at the the top of which is the Linen Hall Cheese Mart, which is well supplied at the fairs, held six times during the year, with cheese from the dairies of Cheshire and North Wales.

We now ascend a handsome gateway called

THE WATERGATE.

the custody of which formerly belonged to the Earls of Derby, who held a valuable river jurisdiction, in executing the mayor's warrants on the Dee, which formerly flowed close underneath. It was purchased from the Derby family by the corporation in

1778, and taken down in 1788, and the present structure erected in 1789, the expense being defrayed out of the murage duties fund. It consists of a wide and lofty arch, thrown over the Watergate-street, where a rapid descent adds much to its apparent elevation. The west side bears the following inscription :

IN THE XXIX YEAR OF THE REIGN OF GEO. III. IN THE
MAYORALTY OF JOHN HALLWOOD, AND JOHN LEIGH, ESQUIRES,
THIS GATE WAS ERECTED.

THOMAS COTGREAVE, } ESQUIRES, MURENGERS.
EDWARD BURROWS,

The view from the summit of this gate is very extensive, the objects immediately surrounding adding much to the pleasure of the scene. On the opposite shore is Curzon Park, with its beautiful villa residences. On the left is Grosvenor Bridge with its far-famed noble arch, the widest circular arch in the world; a little beyond may be seen the grand lodge entrance to Eaton Park, erected at the cost of £14,000. The *tout ensemble* forming a most animating picture. The site of the present Crane-street and the parts adjacent were formerly under water.

Immediately below is the beautiful and spacious lawn called the

ROODEYE.

It contains about 84 statute acres of land, and is let by the corporation as a pasture for cattle. It was once the arena for sports of the Roman soldiery, and the city games and gymnastics were afterwards celebrated here, respecting which there are many curious records extant. Of these, however, the horse races alone remain, which continue to be held on the first week of May, and in the month of October, and enjoy a high reputation on the turf. The course is little more than a mile, and affords the spectators the singular advantage of their being enabled to see the horses during the whole race. The Cheshire Yeomanry assemble annually on the Roodeye for exercise.

The antiquity of the Chester races appears from the following extract from the collection of the late Mr. Nicholls of Chorlton, to whose researches the authors of the History of Cheshire are much indebted. The MS. from which this is extracted, is entitled—

Certayme collections of anciante times, concerning the anciante and famous cittie of Chester, collected by that Reverend Man of God, Mr. Robert Rogers, bachelor of divinitie, archdeacon of Chester, parsone of Gooseworth, and prebande in the Cathedral of Chester, being put in scattered notes, and by his son reduced into these chapters following :—

OF ST. GEORGE'S RACE, OF LATE TIME INVENTED, AND WHEN ALTERED.

"In A. D. 1609, Mr. William Lester, mercer, beinge mayor of Chester, one Mr. Robert Amerye, ironmonger, sometime sherife, of

Chester, (A. D. 1608,) he, with the assent of the mayor and cittie, at his own coste chiefly, as I conceive chiefly, caused three silver cupps of goode value, to be made, the which saide silver cupps were, upon St. George's daye, for ever to be thus disposed : all gentlemen that would bringe their horses to the Rood-dee that daye, and there run, that horse which with spede did over-rune the reste, shoulde have the beste cuppe there presently delivered, and that horse which came seconde, next the firste, before the reste, had the seconde cuppe, there also delivered ; and for the thirde cuppe, it was to be run for at the ringe, by any gentleman that woulde rune for the same, upon the said Rood-dee, and upon St. George's daye ; being thus decreed, that every horse putt in soe much monie as made the value of the cupps or bells, and had the money, which horses did winne the same, and the use of the cupps, till that daye twelve month, beinge in bonde to deliver in the cupps that daye ; soe also for the cuppe for the ringe, which was yearly continued accordingly, until the yeare of our Lord 1623 ; John Brereton, inn-holder, being mayor of Chester, he altered the same after this manner, and caused the three cupps to be sould, and caused more money to be gathered and added, soe that the intereste thereof would make one faire silver cuppe, of the value of £8 as I suppose, it maye be more worth, and the race to be altered, viz. from beyonde the New Tower a great distance and soe to rune five times from that place rownd about the Rood-dee, and he that over-came all the reste the last course, to have the cuppe freely for ever, then and there delivered, which is continued to this daye. But here I must not omit the charge, and the solemnitie made the first of St. George's daye ; he had a poet, one Mr. Davies, who made speeches and poeticale verses, which were delivered at the high crosse, before the mayor and aldermen, with shews of his invention, which booke was imprinted and presented to that famous Prince Henry, eldeste sonne to the blessed King James, of famous memorie. Alsoe he caused a man to go upon the spire of St. Peter's steeple in Chester, and by the fane, at the same tyme he sounded the drum, and displayed a banner upon the top of the same spire. And this was the original of St. George's race with the change thereof, as it is now used.

On the west side of the Roodeye stands

THE HOUSE OF INDUSTRY,

built by the corporation in 1757, as a refuge for age and in-digence. Warm and cold baths are established for the use of the inmates, whose comfort is most studiously consulted and provided for. Behind the house is an establishment for the reception of lunatics. The pleasant row of houses on the right of the Roodeye, is called Paradise Row, the site of which, as appears by an ancient map, was once the deepest part of the river.

Soon after passing the Watergate, on the left, there is a commodious opening to the city, called Smith's Walk, at the bottom of which stands a large house, on the site of which formerly stood the Priory of White Friars or Carmelites.

On the north side of the open field on the left, is a beautiful mansion, now occupied by the Rev. F. Ayckbowm, the re-spected rector of Trinity, but formerly the residence of the late Thomas Harrison, Esq. the celebrated architect, who has immortalized his genius in some of the finest works of which Chester can boast. Near this spot once stood a Convent of Benedictine Nuns, dedicated to St. Mary. It was suppressed with the other lesser monasteries in 1537, and no vestige of the ancient building now remains.

Before proceeding further on our circuit round the walls, we recommend the visitor to turn off to the right, for the purpose of inspecting the

NEW CEMETRY,

which has recently been opened on the other side of the bridge. It is arranged with admirable taste, and was rendered necessary by the overcrowded state of the parochial burial grounds. Opposite the Cemetry gates is a suspension bridge for foot passengers to Curzon Park, from whence we have a fine panoramic view of Chester.

We now retrace our steps to survey that magnificent structure

THE CASTLE.

We have no precise authority whereby to ascertain the date of the foundation of Chester Castle. Some think there is good reason to believe it to be of Roman origin, and of equal antiquity with the city walls. Others have fixed the date of its erection A.D. 1069, by William the Conqueror; but there are some considerations which seem to point to an earlier period than this. It is stated by Camden to have been *repaired* by Hugh Lupus, and additional fortifications erected by the Norman Earls his successors. It was certainly the palace of the local monarchs, as well as their chief stronghold, and retained much of this mixed character until modern alterations were made. Pennant describes the castle as it formerly stood as being composed of two parts—an upper and a lower, each with a strong gate, defended by a round bastion on each side, with a ditch and draw-bridges.

In 1237, upon the death of John Scott, the last earl of the Norman line, the Commissioners of Henry III. seized Chester Castle for the King.

In 1265, James De Aldithley and Urian De St. Pierre, at the head of the citizens of Chester, besieged Luke De Taney, the King's Justice, in the Castle, which held out for ten weeks, when, upon receiving intelligence of the battle of Evesham, he surrendered.

Henry of Lancaster, (afterwards Henry IV.) having taken up arms against Richard II. in 1399, mustered his army upon the bank of the Dee, under the walls of Chester, and Sir Piers

D

Legh of Lyme, an adherent of Richard, was beheaded, and his head
set upon the top of the highest tower in the Castle. Shortly afterwards, the unfortunate Richard and the Earl of Salisbury were
brought prisoners to Chester, mounted (says Hall) " upon two
little nagges, not worth forty franks," when the King was delivered " to the Duke of Gloucester's sonne and the Earle of
Arundell's sonne, that loved him but a little, for he had put
their fathers to death, who led him strait to the castell."

In 1403, Henry Percy, surnamed Hotspur, visited Chester
on his way to the fatal field of Shrewsbury, and caused proclamation to be made, that King Richard was yet alive, and a
prisoner in Chester Castle, where he might be seen.

Eleanor Duchess of Gloucester, wife of the *Good Duke Hum-
phrey*, was confined for several months in Chester Castle, in
1447, previous to her removal to the Isle of Man, under a sen-
tence of perpetual imprisonment on a charge of "practising the
King's death."

Here, in 1651, the Puritans " *sought the Lord*" by trying and
condemning to death the gallant and patriotic Earl of Derby, Sir
Timothy Featherstonehaugh, and Captain Benbow.   According
to Whitlocke, the Earl " attempted to escape, and was let down
by a rope from the leads of his chamber; but some hearing a
noise, made after him, and he was re-taken upon Dee bank."

We shall now proceed to describe the present appearance
and condition of the Chester Castle.   The ancient structure
was taken down at the close of the last century, and the
present magnificent edifice erected on its site.

The principal entrance is through a handsome portico of
Grecian Doric architecture. It is 103 feet by 35, and consists
of a centre and two wings connected by covered passages.
The ten fluted columns, which compose the peristyle in the
centre, are each cut out of a single block of stone. "It is
situated in the centre of a semicircular sunk fence or foss, 13
feet deep, and 390 feet in diameter, cased with hewn stone,
surmounted with stone pedestals at equal distances, and the
spaces filled with handsome iron rails, forming the north
west boundary of the esplanade.*

On the western side of the esplanade, is the Armoury, capable of containing between 30,000 and 40,000 stand of arms.
This is well worthy the inspection of strangers, who cannot
fail to be struck with the excellent state in which the military
stores are kept, and the tasteful arrangement of the arms.

Within the gate at the east end of this range of building,
is the guard-house, behind which is a venerable tower, called

* Pigott's History of Chester.

Julius Agricola's, or *Cæsar's,* which is still entire, and partly occupied as a magazine. Within this tower is a curious chapel, mentioned in the tax-book of Henry VIII. as the chantry "*infra Castrum Cestriæ*" and yielding as its tenth 10s. 8d. It is an upper chamber, about 19 feet by 16, and 16 feet in height. The roof, which is vaulted and groined, is of stone. On one side is a plain pointed recess in the wall, the back of which appears to have been ornamented with paintings, and was probably the altar. James II. heard mass in this chapel.

Returning through the gate we next come to

THE NEW GAOL AND COUNTY HALL.

The principal entrance to the latter is through a portico of twelve columns in double rows, 22 feet high, and 3 feet 1½ inches in diameter, each formed of a single stone. The ceiling, roof, and covering are also of stone. The hall is of a semi-circular form, measuring 80 feet by 50, including the judgment seat, and 44 feet high, and is lighted from above. The ceiling is a semi-dome boldly caissoned with ventilators opening to the roof, in the shape of ornamental roses. It is supported by a row of twelve Ionic columns, each composed of a single stone, from the basis of which there is a gradual descent by a flight of circular steps to the bar, which enables every one in the body of the court to have a perfect view of the judges, counsel, prisoners, and witnesses. There is a subterraneous passage from the dock to the prison, which affords both facility and safety in the removal of the prisoners.

On the right of the entrance to the County Hall are the Grand Jury Room, the Prothonotary's Offices, and the Record Room of the County Palatine, in which some very curious ancient documents are preserved. In a small room on the ground floor is the model of the New Bridge before mentioned, and full length portraits of William III, Charles II, George I, George II, and Frederick Prince of Wales.

On the left is the entrance to the County Gaol, which may vie in every respect with any other establishment of the sort in the kingdom. It is built upon two levels. On the east side of the range of buildings on the upper level is the Deputy Governor's house; adjoining are the day and sleeping rooms of the male debtors, with a large and commodious yard, command-ing a picturesque view of the surrounding country; and in an extensive wing, built a few years ago, are the convicts' cells; apartments for the female debtors and prisoners, with the matron's house and hospital. In the centre, projecting beyond the level, and of a semi-circular form, so as to command a view of the court yards, &c., are the gaolor's or governor's apartments.

Underneath the governor's apartments, and of the same form, is the chapel. It is situate between the upper and lower level, and so ingeniously contrived as to receive the debtors and criminals into different compartments, from their respective court yards. Divine service is performed in the chapel every morning during the week, and twice every Sunday. Rev. H. S. Joseph is the present chaplain, who is most indefatigable in the discharge of his duties. On the lower level, under the jailor's house, are the felons' yards, five in number. They are spacious and airy, and each contains a pump and trough. A sort of area or passage surrounds these yards, and beyond that is the outside wall, built of immense blocks of stone, and conveying at once the idea of security and solidity. Nothing can exceed the excellent discipline and general arrangement of the prisoners. Each has his separate sleeping room, and a commodious day-room is attached to each of the yards. There are distinct cells for solitary confinement and condemned criminals; and convenient cold and warm baths, in which every prisoner is obliged to undergo an ablution upon his entering the prison. His clothes are then taken from him, steamed and stoved, and carefully put away for him to wear on his trial, while he is accommodated with a comfortable suit of the prison uniform in the mean time. A large proportion of the prisoners are profitably employed under the superintendence of a task-master. They are chiefly employed in calico, rug, and carpet weaving, shoe-making, and basket-making. The greater part of the articles of clothing and bed furniture used within the walls are manufactured by them; and the store-room presents the appearance of a complete depository of useful articles for the prison, of almost every description.

There is also a commodious school-room which is efficiently superintended. Every thing relating to the internal management of this prison is complete in each department, and reflects the highest credit on the governor, Mr. Dunstan, who is supreme within the walls, and holds his office by patent from the Crown.

Previous to the present new erections, on the east side of the lower court stood the ancient Shire Hall, in which the courts of justice for the county used to be held. It was a magnificent building, nearly ninety feet in length, and forty-five in breadth; the height very lofty, and worthy the state apartment of the first Norman Earl, Hugh Lupus, who required a hall suitable to the greatness of his hospitality. Adjoining to this hall was the Court of Exchequer, or Court of Chancery, of the county palatine of Chester. It was the Parliament House of the little kings of the palatinate, and had neat gothic seats for the abbot and eight barons.

The east side of the esplanade is appropriated to Barracks, which

contain excellent accommodations for 150 men and their officers.
Behind the Barracks is the Provost, with an enclosed yard
It is no longer employed for this purpose, having been, some
time since, converted into an armoury for pensioners, military
library and reading room, &c. This wing, and the opposite one
on the west side of the esplanade, were built at the joint expense of the Crown and the County Palatine.

Proceeding through the gate at the east end, we come to
THE SESSIONS HOUSE,

A neat and commodious edifice with a tolerably spacious court,
magistrates' and grand jury rooms, and a robing room for counsel
on the ground floor, and up stairs are the Clerk of the Peace's
record rooms and other offices.

Having completed our view of the Castle, we return to continue our walk on the Walls, proceeding onward until we reach
the boundary of the castle walls, where the tourist will have
a splendid view of

GROSVENOR BRIDGE.

This stupendous work of art, which is unequalled in the history
of bridge-building, crosses the Dee at the south-east angle of
the Roodeyé, and is approached by a new road from the centre
of Bridge Street, which passes by the Castle esplanade, proceeds
across the City Walls, and then by an immense embankment,
thrown over a deep valley, to the foot of the bridge. The bridge
consists of one main stone arch, with a small dry arch or towing
path on each side, by which the land communication is preserved
on both sides of the river. The cost of erection was £36,000.

The great distinguishing feature of this edifice is the un-
paralleled width of the chord or span of the main arch, which
is of greater extent than that of any other ever known to have
been constructed. Of its dimensions the following is an accurate
delineation :—The span of the arch, *two hundred feet.** Height
of the arch from the springing line, 40 feet. Dimensions of
the main abutments, 48 feet wide by 40, with a dry arch as a
towing path at each side, 20 feet wide, flanked with immense
wing walls, to support the embankment. The whole length of
the road-way, 340 feet. Width of the bridge from outside the
parapet walls, 35 feet 6 inches, divided thus : carriage road,
24 feet ; the two causeways, 9 feet ; thickness of the parapet
walls, 2 feet 6 inches. Altitude from the top of the parapet
wall to the river at low water mark, 66 feet 6 inches. The
architectural plan of this bridge was furnished by the late Thos.

* The largest stone arch known, that which bears the nearest approach, is at Vieille Briode, which crosses the river Allien, in France,
whose span is 183 feet, being 17 feet less than the Chester bridge. It was
erected in 1454, by Grenier.

Harrison, Esq., contractor and builder; Mr. James Trubshaw, of Staffordshire; surveyor, Mr. Jesse Hartley, of Liverpool. The first stone was laid on the 1st October, 1827, by the late Marquis of Westminster, and a specimen of each of the current coins of the realm deposited therein; and was formally opened in October, 1832, by her Royal Highness the Princess Victoria, her present Most Gracious Majesty, on occasion of her visit, and that of her royal parent, the Duchess of Kent, to Eaton Hall. As an equally delicate and well-merited compliment to her noble host, at the request of the commissioners, the bridge was named "Grosvenor Bridge," by the young Princess. It was opened to the public in December, 1833.

It was near this part of the Walls where King Edgar's palace was situated, from which he was rowed in 971, up the river, to St. John's Priory, by eight tributary princes.

Within seventy yards of the bridge formerly stood an ancient Roman gateway in the walls called the SHIPGATE, or *Hole in the Wall*, at one time the only entrance into Chester from Handbridge. It was taken down some years ago, and is now in the possession of John Finchett Maddock, Esq. It forms a perfect specimen of Roman masonry, originally 20 feet in height by 16 in breadth. Pennant remarks, "that this postern seems originally to have been designed for the common passage over the Dee into the country of the Ordovices, either by means of a boat at high water, or by a ford at low, the river here being remarkably shallow." Opposite the Shipgate is a ford in the river leading through to a field on the Handbridge side, called *Edgar's Feld*, in which stands the ancient sculpture of the *Diva Armigera* PALLAS, already mentioned under the head of ROMAN ANTIQUITIES in a former part of this work.

Pursuing our walk, we next arrive at

THE BRIDGEGATE,

A handsome arch gateway, having two posterns, erected in 1782, at the expense of the corporation. On the tablet over the western postern is the following inscription :—

> THIS GATE WAS BEGUN APRIL, MDCCLXXXII, PATISON ELLAMES, ESQ., MAYOR, AND FINISHED DECEMBER THE SAME YEAR, THOMAS PATISON, ESQ., MAYOR.
>
> THOS. COTGREAVE, ESQ. ⎫ MURENGERS.
> HENRY HESKETH, ESQ. ⎭
>
> JOSEPH TURNER, ARCHITECT.

On another tablet on the east side—

> THIS GATE HAVING BEEN LONG INCONVENIENT, WAS TAKEN DOWN A.D. MDCCLXXXI.
>
> JOSEPH SNOW, ESQ., MAYOR.
>
> THOS. AMERY, ⎫ TREASURERS.
> HENRY HEGG, ⎭

From the top of this gateway the banks of the Dee, with the Bridge, and suburbs of Handbridge, present a lively and striking appearance, which at low water is increased by the rapid falling of the stream over the causeway across the river immediately above the bridge. In the distance may be seen Beeston Castle, on its lofty summit; and the successive ranges of Bucklow and Peckforton Hills, form an impressive and beautiful back-ground.

A little southward stands

THE OLD BRIDGE,

which is of considerable antiquity. A wooden bridge was erected on the same spot by the Mercian Princess Ethelfleda, early in the 10th century; but from the *Chronicle of Chester Abbey*, we learn that in 1227 "pons Cestriæ totus cecedit;" and that in 1279, "mare erupit, pontem Cestriæ confregit et asportavit." The wooden bridge being thus disposed of, we next find from the *Red Book of St. Werburgh*, that "in 1280 the King (Edward I.) compelled the citizens of Chester to rebuild Dee Bridge at their own charge, contrary to the privileges which had been granted to them." In 1500, the south end of the Bridge having fallen into decay was rebuilt, and a tower for its defence added at the entrance into Handbridge, which was taken down about sixty years ago. In 1826 the Bridge was widened to the extent of seven feet, by the addition of a flagged footpath, on the east side, bounded towards the river by a good iron railing, the projection supported by two courses of corbels.

It consists of seven irregular arches, and when viewed from

the west, presents an appearance of venerable antiquity; but on the east it no longer holds out that recommendation to the eye of the observer, modern alterations having left nothing on that side, to render it worthy of notice.

At the north end of the Bridge stand the DEE MILLS, used for the grinding of corn. Although the date of the first erection of mills on this spot cannot now be ascertained, yet there is evidence of their having been there from remote antiquity. Sir Howell-y-Fwyall obtained a grant of them from Edward III. in reward for his services at the battle of Poictiers. In the 5th of Edward VI. they were granted by the Crown to Sir Richard Cotton in exchange for the manors of Bourne and Moreton in Lincolnshire; and by his son George they were granted in fee farm to Edmund Gamul at an yearly rent of £100. Gamul expended a large sum in repairing the causeway originally erected by Hugh Lupus. In 1646 an order of Parliament was issued that the mills and causeway should be destroyed, as an obstruction to trade;—but this order, issued by the Puritans then in power, probably with no other view than to obtain a *composition* from the proprietor, was never complied with. On the alienation of the Gamul property, the greater part of the mills fell into the hands of Mr. Edward Wrench, in whose successor the property of the whole is now vested. The Dee Mills have been twice destroyed by fire within the last sixty years. The first conflagration broke out about twelve at night of Saturday, September 26, 1789; the second, about the same hour of Saturday night, March 6, 1819; on which latter occasion the progress of the flames was so rapid, that the whole of the premises, with the exception of part of the outward wall, were destroyed in less than six hours. The loss sustained was upwards of £40,000. A third fire took place in January, 1847, which destroyed the whole of one of the mills.

We shall now proceed to notice

THE OLD BRIDGEGATE,

which appears to have been of equal antiquity with the bridge itself, for it is shewn by documents in the possession of the Earl of Shrewsbury, that Randle, Earl of Chester, confirmed a gift of his Countess to Poyns, her servant, of the custody of this gate. And another deed of the 13th century, preserved among the same documents, records "quod ego Ricardus Bagoth de Cestr : dedi et omnino quietam clamavi Philippo clerico civi Cestr : *totum jus meum in porta pontis Cestr :* cum omnibus pertinentijs suis." From Philip the clerk the custody of this gate passed to the family of Raby, one of whom, Philip de Raby, in the 14th century had also the keeping of the Earl's garden at the Castle, for which service he received the fruit of a tree called "*a restynge tre*," and whatever remained on the other trees after the first shaking, under the *reddendo* of furnishing the Earl's household with colewort from Michaelmas to Lent, and with leeks during Lent. From the Rabys the custody of the Bridgegate passed to the Norris's, of Speke, in Lancashire, and the Troutbecks. In 1624 the corporation purchased the

THE OLD BRIDGEGATE.

moiety belonging to the Norris's; and in 1660 they also pur-chased the other moiety from the Earl of Shrewsbury, repre-sentative of the Troutbecks, the Earl reserving to himself, during his visits to Chester, the use of a suite of apartments in a house near the gate.

The Old Gate consisted of an arched gateway, flanked with two strong round towers, on one of which was erected a lofty octagonal tower, containing a cistern for supplying the city with water, called Tyrer's Water Works, concerning which Webb says, " The Bridgegate hath of late been greatly beautified by a seemly water-work of stone, built steeple-wise, by the ingenious industry and charge of a late worthy member of the city, John

ANOTHER VIEW OF THE OLD BRIDGEGATE.

Tyrer, gent., and hath served ever since to great use, for the conveying of the river water from the cistern, in the top of that work, to the citizens' houses in almost all the parts of the city, in pipes of lead and wood, *to their no small contentment and commodity.*" The whole fabric was taken down in 1781.

Proceeding eastward, a most pleasing view of the Dee, of considerable extent, is presented before us, with delightful cottage residences on the Boughton bank On the left of the river is a cool and shady walk called *The Groves*, where there are excellent pleasure boats for the accommodation of those who enjoy a sail

up the river. We have here a very good view of St. John's
Church on the right, a venerable pile, containing some very
curious specimens of Saxon architecture.

Within about fifty yards of the Recorder's steps, the wall
forms an angle to the northward. Here we ascend six flights
of steps, consisting of three steps each, called the *Wishing Steps*,
erected in 1785, at the top of which stood an ancient Watch
Tower, which had formerly an apartment with a stone seat on
one side, and windows commanding a view of the river and
adjacent country. This room was removed in 1826.

We next arrive at

THE NEWGATE,

a plain arched gateway, forming a communication betwixt Newgate Street and Pepper Street within the Walls, and St. John's
Street, Dee Lane, &c., without. On the spot now occupied by
this gate, formerly stood a postern, called *Wolf's Gate*, or *Pepper
Gate*. Of this postern, Fuller says, that in the sixteenth century
"the Mayor of the city had his daughter, as she was playing
at ball with other maidens in Pepper Street, stolen away by
a young man through the same gate, whereupon he caused it
to be shut up," which gave rise to the saying, "When the

daughter is stolen, shut Pepper Gate." The postern was removed and the Newgate erected in 1608. From a Journal of
the Siege of Chester, in *King's Vale Royal*, it appears that on
the 29th September, 1645, "the besiegers made a breach in
the walls near to the Newgate, by the battery of 150 cannon
shot, and at midnight made a sharp assault upon the breach.
They likewise attempted to mount the walls with scaling ladders,
but some officers and several soldiers, were hauled in over the
walls; some of the ladders too were dragged over, and many
of the assailants thrown down and killed, and the rest forced
to give over the attack."

A short way further to the eastward, after passing the scanty
remains of an old tower abutting from the Walls, called *Thim-
bleby's Tower*, we arrive at a flight of steps leading to the
Wesleyan Methodist Chapel in St. John's Street, the access to
which from this quarter was made under the sanction of the
corporation. This handsome and commodious place of worship
was erected in 1811. Near to the chapel, is a large and
commodious School-house, recently erected, capable of containing from 200 to 300 children, which is occupied during
the week as a Day School, and is in a prosperous condition.

A few paces now brings us to

THE EASTGATE,

consisting of a wide and beautiful centre arch for the passage
of carriages, and two posterns for the safety and convenience
of foot passengers. It was built at the sole expense of the late
Marquis of Westminster, whose arms, and those of the city,

occupy the centre of the principal arch. On the 8th August,
1768, the south-west corner stone of the Eastgate was laid by
John Page, Esq., Provincial Grand Master, attended by four
regular lodges of Free Masons; and the north-west corner stone
by the Mayor, Sheriffs, and Aldermen of Chester. On the east
side, under the Grosvenor armorial bearings, is the following
inscription :—

ERECTED AT THE EXPENSE OF
RICHARD LORD GROSVENOR,
MDCCLXIX.

And on the west side, under the city arms,

BEGUN A. D. MDCCLXVIII, JOHN KELSALL,
ESQ., MAYOR. FINISHED A. D. MDCCLXIX,
CHAS. BOSWELL, ESQ., MAYOR.

From the summit of this gate there is a fine view of Eastgate
Street, within the walls, and Foregate, or Forest Street on the
outside. On a market day it is truly spirit-stirring to observe
the multitude beneath, and listen to the "busy hum of men,"
citizens and country folks, engaged in buying and selling,—
bringing in and carrying out,—the various commodities which
furnish forth the provision market of a county town.

On the same spot formerly stood

THE OLD EASTGATE,

removed in 1768, as too narrow and inconvenient for one of the
principal entrances to the city. It consisted of a beautifully

formed Gothic archway, flanked by two massive octagonal embattled towers, connected by a substantial building, two storeys
in height, over the gateway, the roof of which was raised to a
level with and embattled in the same manner as the flanking
towers to which it formed the centre. From the bearings on
four shields which ornamented the front of this gate, it is conjectured to have been erected during the reign of Edward III.

A Roman gateway appears to have occupied the same spot
at a still earlier period; for in pulling down the Old Eastgate
in 1768, two wide circular arches of Roman architecture were
discovered within its workmanship.

With all due admiration for the spirit of useful improvement
which dictated the erection of the present Eastgate, we cannot
avoid expressing our regret that the old one no longer remains
to gratify the eye of the antiquary and the man of taste.
Although the present gate is undoubtedly much better adapted
for the entrance of carriages of all kinds, yet the Cestrians of
the last century, who remembered the glories of the old structure must have been but ill reconciled to its substitute.

Having thus completed the circuit of the Walls of Chester,
as they at present stand, it only remains to notice that there
was formerly an outer gate in Foregate Street, about half a
mile from the Eastgate, called

THE BARS GATE,

which, being in a very dilapidated state, was removed as a
nuisance in 1770. An out-work, in connexion with this gate,
was raised previous to the seige of Chester in 1643. This out-
work, consisting of a mud wall, fortified with mounts and

bastions, joined the City Wall at the New Tower, from whence it stretched out to the north-east so far as to take in Upper Northgate Street, then running eastward encompassed all the suburbs on the north of Foregate Street, until it approached Boughton, when it turned southward, and proceeded in that direction across Foregate Street at the Bars Gate, down Dee Lane, at the bottom of which its course was terminated by the river. This outwork withstood a violent assault by the Puritans under Sir Wm. Brereton, on the 18th July, 1643, wherein the assailants were forced to retire with great loss; but on the 19th of September, 1645, it was surprised and carried by a night assault of the enemy, under the command of General Louthian, and was afterwards occupied by the Puritans as a circumvalla-tion, while prosecuting the siege of the city.

"In perusing the foregoing sketch of our Walls, with the incidental notices of contiguous objects, it is presumed, that individuals, most con-versant with the localities of the city, will meet with several particulars, either to gratify their curiosity, or add to their information. And it may also be hoped, that should the account be read by those who are strangers to our ancient fortifications, and the peculiar attractions of Chester, it may excite a commendable inquisitiveness for a personal survey, at the same time that it may assist as a directory to their inquiries. In whatever point of view these old ramparts are considered, they possess an imposing interest, and confer incalculable benefits. To the invalid, the sedentary student, or the man of business, occupied during the day in his shop or counting-house; to the habitually indolent, who require excitement to necessary exercise, to all these, the promenade on Chester Walls, have most inviting attractions, where they may breathe all the salubrious winds of heaven in a morning or an evening walk. Here the enthusiastic anti-quarian, who would climb mountains, ford rivers, explore the bowels of the earth, and, regardless of toil and the claims of nature, exhaust his strength in search of a piece of rusty cankered brass, or a scrap of Roman earthenware, can scarcely advance a dozen paces but the pavement on which he treads, or some contiguous object, forces upon his observation the reliques of times of earliest date. Nor can the philosophic moralist encompass our venerable walls without having his mind, comparing the splendid and gigantic works of antiquity with their present condition, strongly impressed with the mutations produced by the lapse of ages, and the perishing nature of all mundane greatness.

I shall conclude this branch of our History by citing the sentiments of a man well known to the republic of letters, regarding our ancient city, not indeed particularly as to her walls, but as to her general attractions. His information as a traveller was varied and extensive, and his discern-ment and intellect strong and acute. This gentleman, who was no other than Mr. Boswell, in a letter to Dr. Johnson, dated October 22, 1779, says, 'Chester pleases me more than any town I ever saw. I told a very pleasing young lady, niece to one of the Prebendaries (Miss Letitia Barnston) at whose house I saw her, 'I have come to Chester, madam, I cannot tell how; and far less can I tell how to get away from it." Dr. Johnson in reply says, 'In the place where you are, there is much to be observed, and you will easily procure yourself skilful directors.' In another letter, dated November 7, in the same year, Boswell remarks, 'I was quite enchanted at Chester, so that I could with difficulty quit it.'"*

* Hemingway's History of Chester.

A WALK THROUGH THE CITY.

IT is our purpose now to conduct the tourist through the city, that we may point out in detail, the various objects of interest which claim his attentive inspection. But before commencing our perambulations through the principal streets, we will here introduce a few remarks on that unique feature which constitutes the distinguishing attraction of Chester, and has given it universal celebrity,

THE ROWS.

Very curious are these old arcades, which are as interesting to the antiquarian as they are convenient for a quiet lounge to ladies and others engaged in shopping. They occupy the greatest part of both sides of Eastgate Street, and the upper parts of both

EASTGATE ROW NORTH.

sides of Watergate Street and Bridge Street. Those in Northgate Street are more irregular, only one side, commonly called Shoemakers' Row, being used as a regular thoroughfare. Their appearance, both interior and exterior, are extremely singular. They form a gallery, occupying the front floor of each house, parallel with the streets below, and are approached by flights of steps, placed at convenient distances, in addition to those by which they are entered and quitted at each end. The passenger walks over the shops on a level with the street, and under the first floor of the dwelling-houses, and thus two lines of shops are erected in one front. The rows are kept in excellent repair, and form the chief promenade of the citizens. To strangers they cannot fail to prove an object of curiosity. Whilst these rows are exceedingly singular, they are also often found to be very convenient, as in weather they afford ample protection from the "pitiless storm." The shops in the rows are generally considered the best situations for retail shop-keepers; but those on the southern side of Eastgate Street and the eastern side of Bridge Street have a decided preference. Shops let here at high rents, and are in never-failing request; and perhaps there are no parts of the city which have undergone equally rapid or extensive improvements.

In the sixteenth century they appear not to have exceeded 6 feet in height and 10 in width, with clumsy wooden rails towards the street, and large oaken pillars, supporting transverse beams and brackets, on which rested the houses over head, formed of wood and plaster, so far over-hanging the street that in some places the upper floor of opposite houses nearly met. Nearly the whole of the buildings of this description are now taken down; and in re-building care has been taken to raise and widen the rows, and to place iron railings towards the street in place of the wooden posts formerly used. The shops in the rows present a very different appearance to that of about 60 years ago; then, as Hemingway says, "the fronts were all *open* to the row in two or three compartments, according to their size; and at night were closed by large hanging shutters fixed on hinges, and fastened in the day time by hooks to the ceiling of the row." At present these rows are "capable of supplying all the real demands of convenience and the artificial calls of luxury, mental and corporeal, presenting a cluster of drapers, clothiers, jewellers, booksellers, &c., as respectable as the kingdom can produce." *

The origin and cause of the rows has furnished matter for much curious investigation; and many conflicting conjectures have been propounded respecting them. The subject is involved in much obscurity; and in the absence of any positive data, we are not able to take higher ground than the probabilities of the case. It has been alleged that they were originally used as places of defence, from whence to annoy and repulse the assaults of the enemy, who might gain entrance into the streets beneath,

* Hemingway's History of Chester.

E

by surprising the gates during those remote ages, when Chester was subject to the sudden incursions of the Welsh. But against this opinion it may be urged, that in no one of their attacks upon this city did the Welsh ever force their way within the gates or walls; so that these latter, being proved by experience to be a sufficient bulwark against our foes, there existed no necessity for the erection of any further defences. There is irrefragable evidence that the *form* of our city is Roman, and that our *walls* were the work of that people; and the same reasons which justify these conclusions are not less cogent for presuming that the construction of our streets are Roman also. Pennant appears to have arrived at this conclusion:—he says, "these rows appear to me to have been the same with the ancient *vestibules*, and to have been a form of building preserved from the time that the city was possessed by the Romans. They were built before the doors, midway between the streets and the houses, and were the places where dependants waited for the coming out of their patrons, and under which they might walk away the tedious minutes of expectation. Plautus, in the 3rd act of his *Mostella*, describes both their station and use:—

'Viden vestibulum ante œdus, et ambulacrum ejasmodi.'

The shops beneath the rows were the Cryptæ and Apothecæ, magazines for the various necessaries of the owners of the houses."

Ormerod says that some of these crypts exhibit specimens of vaulting equal to the cloisters of our cathedral.

Camden, in describing Chester, says, "the houses are very fair built, and along the chief streets are galleries or walking places they call rows, having shops on both sides, through which a man may walk dry from one end to the other." And Shukeley, in his Itinerary in 1724, says, "the rows or piazzas are singular through the whole town, giving shelter to foot people. I fancied it a remain of the *Roman porticoes*."

The supposition that their construction is of Roman origin, seems to be the most reasonable one, being sustained by many collateral evidences. In the oldest histories, descriptive of the city in some form or other, the elevated rows and the shops beneath, are recognised; nor have we the slightest intimation of any period in which these rows were constructed, or when the level of the streets were sunk so much below the surface of the walking paths in the rows and the ground behind them. There is no doubt that the pavement in Bridge Street, Watergate Street, and Eastgate Street, were originally on a level with the ground floor of the houses standing in the rows, and that they have been made to take their present form at some period or other, by dint of human art and labour; nor does there appear any reason to doubt, that the excavations by which these singular galleries are distinguished from the carriage road, are the work of Roman hands.

Tacitus, "in describing the process by which Roman manners diffused themselves throughout Britain, and gradually completed the subjugation of the country, speaks of the natives of Britain as acquiring a taste for the two leading features in Roman civilization, "Porticus and Balnea," — the portico in which they were delighted to stroll and sun themselves, and the baths which were their national luxury. He mentions these, and we cannot but be struck, by the coincidence with things, with which we are all familiar—the *Rows* of our ancient city and the Hypocaust which is still shewn as the Roman bath. We are hereby led to infer, that the mode of construction which gives the character to our city, originated in Roman habits.*"

PRINCIPAL STREETS.

Within the walls, the city is subdivided by four principal streets, intersecting each other at right angles at Peter's church, which stands in the centre of the city. These streets retain numerous old timber buildings, which give them an unusual and impressive appearance, and are much wider in general than those of cities of equal antiquity. Immediately in front of the church formerly stood the High Cross, which was pulled down and defaced by the Parliamentarians when they took possession of the city in 1646. The upper portion of this valuable antiquity is still preserved in the grounds of Netherlegh House, though some of the carved figures are a good deal injured. Mr. Pennant is of opinion that St. Peter's church and a few houses to the north and west occupy the site of the *Roman Prætorium*, with its Court of Judicature and Angulale, where prayers, sacrifices, and other religious rites were wont to be performed.

Adjoining the cross formerly stood that ignominious instrument of punishment, called the *Pillory*, which happily, the spirit of the times has long since dispensed with.

Adjoining the south side of St. Peter's church, stood the old Pentice, where the magistrates performed their judicial duties, where the sheriffs sat to determine civil causes, and where the Town-office was kept, until the year 1803, when it was removed for the purpose of widening the road into Northgate and Watergate streets, at that time extremely narrow and dangerous. The bench of magistrates was then removed to much more commodious apartments in the Exchange. At the corner of the east of Bridge-street and the west of Eastgate-street and near to the Cross, there was formerly a small stone building, form-

* Rev. Chancellor Raikes.

E 2

ing a basin at the top, called the *Conduit*, to which water was
formerly brought into the city from St. Giles's well at Boughton, and thence conveyed to different parts of the city.*

The Cross used formerly to be the scene of the barbarous
sport of bull-baiting of which the following satirical sketch is
given in an old history of Chester now before us:—

" The Cross is famous for being the annual scene of exhibition of that *polite play* called a bull-bait; where four or five
of these *horned heroes* are attended by several hundred lovers
of that *rational amusement.* Till within a few years, the *dramatis
personæ* of this *elegant scene* included even magistracy itself,
the mayor and corporation attending in their official habiliments, at the Pentice windows, not only to countenance the
diversions of the *ring*, but to participate in a sight of its *enjoy-
ments.* A proclamation was also made, by the crier of the
court, with all the gravity and solemnity of an oration before
a *Romish sacrifice ;* the elegant composition of which run thus,
" *Oyez! Oyez! Oyez! If any man stands within twenty yards
of the bull-ring, let him take—what comes.*" After which followed the usual public ejaculations, for "the safety of the king
and the mayor of the city ;" when the *beauties* of the scene commenced, and the dogs immediately *fell to.* Here a prayer for
his worship was not unseasonable, as even the ermin'd cloak
was no security against the carcases of dead animals, with
which spectators, without distinction, were occasionally saluted.

"We shall not attempt a description of the *tender* offices
practiced, at such times, on so noble a creature—one, however,
we cannot omit mentioning—in 1787, an unfortunate animal,
smarting under his wounds and fatigue, was very *naturally*
induced to *lie down ;*—the *argument* made use of, in this situation, however, *as naturally* induced him to *get up ;*—his *humane* followers hitting upon the ingenious expedient of setting
fire to some straw under his body ; when, it is hardly necessary to add, " the wretched animal heav'd forth such groans,
as stretch'd his leathern coat almost to bursting." This circumstance of the *fire* was, however, no bad *satire* (emblematically
considered) on the transactions of the day—the whole being
little better than a—" burning shame."

"The late Dr. Cowper is said to have had the merit, when
mayor, of putting a stop to the attendance of the corporate
body on these days; and Mr. Alderman Brodhurst, in his
mayoralty, made a laudable, but ineffectual, effort to suppress
a relick of barbarism, 'more honoured in the *breach* than the
observance.'"

* Hemingway's Chester.

EASTGATE STREET,

A spacious street, forming a direct line to the Eastgate, about 209 yards in length. The appearance of the street has been considerably modernized of late years; many of the old houses having been taken down and spacious shops and dwelling-houses erected on their site. There is a very interesting old crypt to be seen on the premises of Messrs. Prichard, Drapers,

EASTGATE STREET.

which furnishes an additional illustration of the statement already made, that many of the buildings in the principal streets are erected on the remains of ancient religious houses. This crypt is supposed to have been erected in the eighth century. Dr. Ormerod gives it as his opinion that these conventual buildings occupied nearly, if not wholly, one fourth of the city. About two-thirds down the street on the right, is Newgate Street, and opposite is St. Werburgh's Street, leading to the Cathedral. There are two excellent Inns in Eastgate Street, the Green Dragon and the

ROYAL HOTEL.

This is a fine lofty edifice, the front resting on six or eight round stone pillars, betwixt which and the coffee-room, there is a capacious piazzi; the front has a commanding appearance, and the accommodations within, are most excellent. Passing under the arch you enter

FOREGATE STREET,

A spacious airy street, about 572 yards in length, and in the most parts 18 in breadth; on the right hand is St. John-street, in which is situated on the left the Post-office, and a little lower down on the right the Mechanics' Institution and News-room. The spacious circular building is a place of worship used by the Wesleyan Methodists. The narrow street on the left takes us to St. John's Church and Priory, which will amply repay a careful and attentive study.

Returning to the Cross we now proceed down

WATERGATE STREET,

Which possesses remarkable interest, from the number of very old houses that are still remaining in it. This street has perhaps suffered less from the innovation of modern improvement than any other part of Chester. The rows on both sides extend nearly to the bottom of the street, and retain several marks of great antiquity. In front of an old house on the south side of the street, there is a post with the date 1539 carved upon it. On the same side, nearer the Cross, is an old dwelling-house, with the inscription—

         "God's Providence is mine Inheritance—1652,"

cut upon a beam in front, in legible characters. At the time when the plague was devastating the city, this was almost the only house which was exempt from its destructive havoc.

Gratefully sensible of this singular blessing, the pious occupier placed this inscription on the front of his house, as a commemorative memorial of Divine Providence and care. Lower down on the same side, is a singularly decorated old house, having the whole front divided into square compartments, filled with carved work of various descriptions, principally heraldry and scripture history. In the lowest line of compartments, immediately over the row, are represented the following subjects:—Adam and Eve standing on each side of the tree of knowledge, the serpent twined round the trunk of the tree, and over head a winged bust, representing, perhaps, an angel issuing from the clouds;—Cain killing Abel;—Abraham offering up Isaac;—Susannah and the Elders;—a naked figure seated on a bed, holding a sword in the right hand, the point towards his side, apparently in the act of committing suicide. There are three other compartments in the same line with those above described, two of them consist of armorial bearings, including the Earldoms of Chester and Derby, &c. crested with a bishop's mitre; the third bears an inscription, illegible from the street, and the date 1613. This house was built by Dr. George Lloyd, of the family of Lloyd of Kinmell, in North Wales, Bishop of Chester from 1604 to 1615.

Lower down, on the same side of the street, below Nicholas Street, is a curious and spacious old palace, once the mansion of the Derby family, which is well deserving of the visitor's notice. It is approached through a narrow passage. The

THE WATERGATE.

front of the house presents some interesting specimens of curious ornamental carved work. On this spot once stood a *Monastery* of the order of Black Friars.

The street on the opposite side leads to the new Linen Hall, where the cheese fairs are periodically held. It was built by the Irish merchants in 1778. At that time the imports of linen were very considerable, and a large business was done.

At the corner of this street stands her Majesty's Custom House, a small, inelegant building, destitute of any outward features to arrest the attention of the passer-by. Adjoining is Trinity Church, which contains the mortal remains of Parnell the poet, and Matthew Henry, immortalized in his far-famed commentary. Trinity Street contains nothing worthy of special notice: it leads, however, to a memorable spot, of surpassing interest to all who love to trace the "records of a good man's life." Higher up is Crook Street, where stands the chapel built for Matthew Henry. These chapel walls once echoed the voice of that eloquent divine, who assiduously defended the principles of a sound protestant, evangelic faith. Associated therefore, as the place is with the memory of a great mind, whose works have taken an honourable position in the religious literature of the country, it cannot but be a great attraction, to all who love to treasure the incidents, which mark the history, of a great and worthy man. Matthew Henry's chapel is now occupied by the Unitarians.

Returning now to the Cross, we proceed to

NORTHGATE STREET,

which forms the northern division of the city, and is 440 yards long. On the east side, adjoining St. Peter's Church, are the Commercial buildings, occupied as a subscription News Room and City Library, which contains an extensive collection of valuable old works. The Rows in Northgate Street are chiefly formed of wood, and retain all the inconveniences of antiquity, unsophisticated by the innovating hand of improvement. That on the west is the only one in general use, extending from the Cross to the Fish Market. The regular market for " Fish and vegetables (says a History of Chester, 1791,) is in the square, opposite the Exchange, which in general are plentiful and reasonable. In that useful article, salmon, no market in the kingdom did, some few years ago, excel it; indeed such was the profusion of this valuable fish, that masters were often restricted, by a clause of indenture, from giving it more than twice a week to their apprentices! Though the bounty of Providence, in this particular, is yet unabated, such restriction is no longer necessary—some *artificial* cause or other, very *kindly* rendering this fish, at the present day, a *delicacy* even to the *masters* themselves."

THE EXCHANGE

is situated in the Market-place, on the west side of Northgate Street. It was commenced in 1695, and completed in 1698, at an expense of £1000, towards which Roger Whitley, then Mayor, contributed largely. It is a noble brick building, ornamented with stone work, supported by stone pillars on the ground floor, through which is a spacious thoroughfare from south to north. In a niche on the south front is a statue of Queen Anne in her coronation robes. On the right of this statue is a tablet, having the arms of the Earldom of Chester on a circular shield in the centre, and above these the coats of the principality of Wales and Duchy of Cornwall, having each their respective coronets over them; beneath are two dragons, *seant regardant*, as supporters. The blazon of this tablet, which is much admired, is believed to have been furnished by the last Randle Holmes, deputy Norroy king at arms, who died in 1707. On the left of the statue is another tablet, containing the Royal Arms of England, as borne by Queen Anne. The statue originally held a sceptre in the right, and a ball in the left hand, but these have long since been destroyed. The ground floor of the Exchange originally consisted of four rows of pillars, having the intervals entirely open. But in 1756, apprehensions being entertained of the stability of these pillars to sustain the floor above, the range of shops on the west side, and the shop at the south-east were erected with a view to strengthen the building. The centre of the building is occupied by the *Common Hall*, wherein are held the city sessions, and where the annual election of the mayor and sheriff takes place. The north end of the Common Hall is fitted up as a court of justice, having a bench, bar, witness and jury boxes. On each side of the bench are ornaments, composed of lictors' fasces, spears, &c., used to support the sword and mace. The walls are hung round with the following portraits :—on the east side Recorders Combermach and Leycester; on the north-east angle Recorder Sir William Williams; and adjoining the last, Sir Henry Bunbury, the city's representative in eight successive parliaments during the reigns of Queen Anne and George the First; and Sir John Grey Egerton, member for the city from 1807 to 1818; at the north-west angle, Recorder Levinge; and on the west side, Recorder Townsend and Thomas Cholmondeley, Esq., Mayor in 1761.

Adjoining and communicating with the Common Hall on the north is the Council Room, commonly called the *Pentice*, where the mayor and magistrates sit three times a week as a Court of

Petty Session.   Over the mayor's seat in this room is a splendid
full length portrait of George the Third in his coronation robes,
the figure by Gainsborough, the drapery by Reynolds, presented
to the city by the late Marquis of Westminster in 1808.   Here
are also full portraits of Robert Earl Grosvenor in his parliamentary robes, painted by Jackson; Richard Earl Grosvenor
and Thomas Grosvenor, Esq., M.P. for the city, in their robes
as Mayors of Chester, painted by West.   On the south side are
the portraits of several distinguished benefactors of the city.
There is also a full length portrait of William Cross, Esq. the first
Mayor after the passing of the Reform Bill.   At the north end
of the Exchange is the Market, appropriated for the sale of
butter; and a few yards apart is another building of equal breadth,
but longer, for butchers' meat, both of which are neatly fitted

THE OLD NORTHGATE.

up and well adapted for their respective purposes. We recommend the tourist now to continue his walk up the street, for the purpose of visiting the Training College, which we doubt not, our former description has made him curious to see. Supposing this to have been done, we now return on the east side, passing through the Northgate about 100 yards, where we come

THE NORTHGATE.

to a narrow avenue on the left under an old archway, the remains of one of the gates of the monastery of St. Werburgh. A little further down, opposite the market hall, stands a noble arch called

THE ABBEY GATE,

which is a Gothic pointed arch with a postern at the side, both of which are included in a larger obtuse one, apparently of the same order. The interior of the gateway is vaulted with stone, with ribs, and carved keystones at the intersections, and the rooms over were originally approached by a spiral staircase.*

* An incident connected with these rooms (says Hemingway), which occurred about fifty years ago, is still remembered, and often spoken of by many of our ancient gossips. A Mr. Speed, the then deputy registrar, had been frail enough to entice a female, as frail as himself, into a room adjoining his office; when an unexpected visitant arriving, who required his immediate presence, for fear of an unlucky discovery, he locked her up in the room. The fair one became so alarmed that she opened one of the windows looking into Abbey Square, from which she threw herself to the ground, but without any serious injury. The whole story, however, soon became known, and the subject of the incident was subsequently illustrated in a humourous caricature, to which was appended the following distich, said to be written by the late Massie Taylor, Esq.—

"Since women are so fond of men,
    With *Speed* she will fly up again."

The copper-plate is in the possession of the publisher of this work, on which is engraved the following inscription :—" A Speed-y method of getting out of the Spiritual Court."

On the south side was the porter's lodge, and on the other St. Thomas's court. Before this gate were anciently raised the booths, for the merchants frequenting the Abbot's fair, these booths were covered with reeds, which the Monks were empowered to gather from Stanlaw Marsh ; and here also the performers in the Chester Mysteries commenced the exhibition of their pageants. This was formerly the grand entrance into the monastery, which appears to have occupied a very extensive range. On passing through the arched gateway we enter into the Abbey Square. On the right hand is a dead wall, enclosing the episcopal palace, which was re-built by Bishop Keene out of his private resources, at an expense of £2200, soon after his promotion to the see in 1752. In former days the residence of the Abbots of St. Werburgh stood on this site. The spacious edifice at the end of the palace wall is the Registry Office, of which Dickens has given an interesting sketch in his "Household Words" in one of his able papers entitled "The Doom of English Wills." The entire arrangements and management of the office are described in terms of unqualified commendation, highly complimentary to the talented registrar, who is described as "a gentleman who fulfills the duties of his office in person with assiduity." In the centre of the square is a neat shrubbery, enclosed with an iron palisading, having in the centre an eliptic column, which was once a pillar under the Exchange ; but on removing it to build a shop there, the corporation presented it to the Dean and Chapter, who appropriated it to its present use. In the north-east angle of the square is the Deanery, built on the site where once stood an old Gothic structure, called St. Thomas' Chapel. Returning into Northgate Street, the next narrow avenue on the left gives us a fine view of the west transept of the Cathedral, with its beautiful window, enriched with elegant tracery. A few paces below we arrive at

THE THEATRE ROYAL.

The citizens of Chester appear to have been early distinguished for a love of theatricals. From a MS. entitled, "Certayne collections of aunchiante times concerninge the aunchiante and famous Citty of Chester," by Archdeacon Rogers, we learn that in the beginning of the 14th century, Randal Higden, a monk of Chester, "translated the Bible into several partes and plays, so as the common people might learne the same by theyre playinge." These *spectacles*, then called the *Whitsun Plays*, were first performed in 1328, during the mayoralty of Sir John Arneway, at the expense of the city companies ; and being "profitable for them, for all both far and near came to see them," they were repeated annually on Monday, Tuesday, and Wednesday, in Whitsun week, for nearly 250 years, until 1574, when they were suppressed by authority. The theatre for these performances was of the original Thespian cast, a four-wheeled scaffold or waggon, whereof the body served for a tyring room, and the roof of the stage, whereon the members of the different city companies did " each man play his part." The first place of performance was at the Abbey Gate, that " the monks and churche might have the first sighte, and then the stage was drawne to the High Crosse before the Mayor and Aldermen, and soe from streete to streete; and when one pageant was ended another came in the place thereof, till all that were appoynted for the daye were ended." Each company had its own peculiar parts allotted to its members to perform in the Whitsun Plays, of which a list is given in the above quoted MS.

In addition to the Whitsun Plays, the citizens were anciently entertained with processional pageants by the different companies, which latter appear to have survived the suppression of the former for many years. They were suppressed for some time by the party in power during the Commonwealth, but revived with great splendour at the Restoration.

The pageants were abolished by order of the Corporation in 1678.

" No circumstance," says the old history from which we have already quoted, " can evince the strange mutations to which things are liable, more than this place : which was originally a *chapel* dedicated to *St. Nicholas*, and devoted to *religion ;* afterwards a *common hall* devoted to *justice ;* next a *warehouse* devoted to *trade ;* and now a *playhouse* devoted to *amusement*."

Returning to the Cross, from whence we set out, we now direct our attention to

BRIDGE STREET,

which is an open and spacious street, in length from the Cross to the Bridge about 554 yards. This street is characterized by many striking features, which will afford deep interest to the antiquarian, and indeed to all who love to visit the localities, which are associated with any remarkable events and phases of our national and ecclesiastical history. Although the buildings now present a much more modern aspect than they did some years ago, there are still remaining many conspicuous proofs of the antiquity of the city, and many curious remains which give it peculiar attractions.

A little way down the street, on the left hand, is a house now occupied by Mr. W. Brittain, Woollen Draper, which is rendered remarkable from a peculiar, and as it resulted, *fortunate*

incident, which occurred there in 1558. In that year Dr.
Cole, Dean of St. Pauls, came to Chester on his way to Ireland, intrusted with a commission from Queen Mary, for
prosecuting the Protestants in that part of the kingdom. The
commissioner stopped one night in this house on his way, then
a noted inn, called the *Blue Posts*, where he was visited by
the Mayor, to whom, in the course of conversation, he commu-
nicated his errand, taking out a leather box out of his cloak bag,
and saying, in a tone of exultation, "Here is what will lash
the heretics of Ireland!" This announcement was overheard
by the landlady of the house, who had a brother in Dublin;
and whilst the commissioner was complimenting his worship
down stairs, the good woman, prompted by a tender regard for
the safety of her brother, opened the box, and taking out the
commission, placed in its stead a pack of cards, with the knave
of clubs uppermost. The unsuspecting Doctor packed up the
box again, and with its far different contents proceeded on

BRIDGE STREET.

his journey. On his arrival at the Castle of Dublin, the
precious box was presented to the Lord Deputy and privy
council, who, on opening it, found, in the place of the commission, the pack of cards, prefaced with the significant *knave of
clubs*. The surprise of the assembly was of course very great,
and the Doctor's perhaps the greatest of all; he was not lack
in his protestations that the commission he *had* received, and was
entirely ignorant how it had disappeared. "Let us have an-

other commission," said the Deputy, and forthwith the amazed and chagrined Commissioner returned to court for the purpose : but before he could return to Ireland, Queen Mary died. Elizabeth, her successor, rewarded the woman, whose name was Elizabeth Edwards, with a pension of £40 a year during her life.

A little lower down, on the same side, are the remains of a Roman Bath and Hypocaust, which we have minutely described under the head of Roman Antiquities. This curious relic, we take for granted, he will "go and see."

A little further is the Church of St. Michael, which has recently been erected on the site of the old church, which had become so much delapidated, that apprehensions were excited as to its safety.

Passing Pepper Street, adjoining St. Michael's, we next meet with

THE ALBION HOTEL,

A capacious building, elegantly fitted up, connected with which is a spacious Assembly Room, and behind the premises extensive pleasure grounds and bowling green. The admirable arrangements and accommodation of this excellent hotel have given it a deservedly high repute.

Passing on to the lower end of the street, we come to St. Olave's Church, an edifice of very mean pretensions, but of very ancient foundation. In the copy of an old Court Roll, the advowson of St. Olave's is mentioned among other advowsons, belonging to the Abbey of St. Werburgh. A clerk was instituted and inducted upon the presentation of the Abbey, in the time of King John.* Continuing down the street we arrive at a handsome arch called the Bridgegate, beyond which is the old bridge, which will lead the tourist (should his curiosity incline him) to Edgar's Cave, already described under the head of antiquities.

Returning on the west side of the street, we come to a steep lane, called St. Mary's Hill, which leads to the Castle and St. Mary's Church.

Opposite St. Olave's Church, before mentioned, is an old house, formerly occupied by the Gamul family, which possesses great interest from the fact of its having given protection to Charles 1st, during the siege of Chester by the Parliamentary forces. There is some very curious painted pannel work and beautiful carving in the interior, which render it well worthy of inspection. A little higher up is an antiquated. building

* Gastrell's Notitia Cestensiensis, vol. 1, p. 110

called "the Falcon Inn;" a fine specimen of the old timber houses of Chester; adjoining this house, formerly stood the

OLD LAMB ROW,

which was one of the most remarkable objects of curiosity in the city. The materials of which the buildings were composed were the same as that of the Falcon, which is probably an older building than the Old Lamb Row was. It was constructed of massy beams of oak, heavy roofs, and the interstices of the timber in the fronts filled up with sticks and clay. The age of the Row is pretty clearly determined by the inscription on a stone, discovered after the fall of the building :—

16—H—55
R. H.

The initials of Randle Holme, the builder. This was the mansion of the family of Holme, the famous Cheshire antiquaries. In the year 1670, the third Randle made some important and obnoxious alterations, which brought upon him the censure of the corporation, who ordered that "the nuisance erected by Randle Holme in his new building in Bridge-street, near to the two churches, be taken down, as it annoys his neighbours, and hinders their prospect from their houses." He proceeded with his work, however, *sans ceremonie*; and in the following year Mr. Holme, painter, "was fined £3 6s. 8d. for contempt to the Mayor, in *proceeding* in his building in Bridge-street." It continued the residence of that heraldic family so late as 1707. It appears that the Holme family subsequently sank into extreme indigence, and at no very distant period, we believe, a descendant was an occasional boots and waiter at a tavern in Liverpool. Such are the reverses of fortune! How this property became alienated from the Holmes, has not been ascertained. It was occupied about the middle of the last century as a public house, called "The Lamb," whence it derived the name of the Lamb Row. In 1821, in the middle of the day, it suddenly gave way and tumbled into the street; happily without any injury to the inhabitants. An old woman was sitting in the upper room at the moment the over-hanging roof bore down the trembling building beneath : the wall of the apartment separated within six inches of a chair on which she was seated, but she fortunately escaped.

After passing Grosvenor-street, we come to White Friars, which derives its name from a monastery of Carmelites or White Friars being once located there. The next turning is Common-hall-street, so called from its being the place where the Common-hall of the city formerly stood, as its name imports. Some are of opinion that it occupied the site of a building now used as a Dissenting chapel; but Ormerod is of opinion that it stood on the *south* side of the street, near to several old alms-houses which still remain.

Prior to the era of the Reformation, Chester abounded in its religious institutions and edifices. We have already indicated this fact, in pointing out the localities where some of these religious buildings were situated. There are many convincing evidences, in the lower part of several houses in the principal streets, that they have been erected on the ruins of these ecclesiastical foundations. A remarkable instance in support of this supposition, has recently been brought to light, upon clearing out an underground cellar behind the shop of Messrs. Powell and Edwards, cutlers, a little further up in the street, when the remains of

AN ANCIENT CHAPEL

were discovered. We are much indebted to the care and good taste of these gentlemen, that this valuable antiquity has been so admirably preserved; and as they are most courteous in affording strangers the privilege of examining it, we doubt not that the opportunity will be gladly taken. The chapel is of an oblong form, running from east to west. Its dimensions are 42 feet in length, 15 feet 3 inches in breadth, and the height, from the surface of the floor to the intersections of the groining of the roof, 14 feet. It was partially lighted through the upper part of the west end, in which there are three small windows, divided by stone mullions, and protected by iron bars. On examining the intersection of the groins, marks were discovered on the stone work, that a couple of lamps had been used for lighting. The entrance to the east end was by a flight of steps cut out of the rock; this passage is now closed, but

F

from what remains, there is no doubt this was the case. On the south side is an Anglo-Norman-Gothic doorway, attained by three or four circular steps, and forms an outlet within its inner and outer wall, by another flight of steps to the surface above the building. At the west end are two niches, on which the baptismal fonts are supposed to have been placed; one of these was found during the excavation, and is deposited in one of these recesses; the other was unfortunately destroyed by the workmen. The date of the erection of this interesting structure is supposed to be early in the 13th century. Taking into consideration the fact that not far from this spot were the monasteries of Grey Friars and White Friars, it has been conjectured by some that in this chapel they assembled for their religious celebrations. It seems to be, however, a more feasible hypothesis, that the site was once occupied by some order of religious house; that the chapel formed a part of the erection, and was used by the inmates for their religious ceremonies and worship. In the upper part of the premises, there appear to be some characteristic remains of the ancient structure. Lacking any further evidence, as to the character and extent of this venerable building, than the place itself supplies, the question is involved in uncertainty. The crypt is a most interesting curiosity, worthy of the investigation of the antiquarian, and to his better judgment we leave the subject.

A VISIT TO THE CATHEDRAL.

REVIOUS to the Roman conquests, the Britons were accustomed to celebrate the rites of Druidism; but as it was the custom of the Romans to carry into the lands they conquered, not only their civil polity but also their religion, the gods of the Pantheon became consequently the gods of our ancestors. Near the existing memorials of Druidical superstition, there arose the majestic fanes of a more polished mythology. At Bath there is said to have been a temple dedicated to Minerva, while on the site now occupied by the splendid cathedral of St. Paul there was a temple to Diana. It appears from a passage in "King's Vale Royal," there was a tradition generally accepted in his day, that on the present site of Chester

Cathedral, was a temple dedicated to Apollo, during the period that the city was inhabited by the Legionaries.

"I have heard it," he says, "from a scholar residing in the city, when I was there, anno 1653, that there was a temple dedicated to Apollo in olden time, in a place adjoining to the Cathedral Church, by the constant tradition of the learned."

We are not aware that the supposition is capable of being verified by any existing record, but when we take into consideration the policy generally pursued by the Romans in subjugating a country, it seems to be countenanced by strong probability. With this form of Paganism, however, there came zealous men, of true apostolic stamp, whose earnest inculcation of vital principles, accelerated the progress of a better faith. So conspicuous had that progress become early in the third century, that Tertullian, in his work written against the Jews, A.D. 209, states that "even those places in Britain, hitherto inaccessible to the Roman arms, have been subdued by the gospel of Christ."

The ground on which the temple of Apollo once stood (if the tradition be trustworthy,) was occupied early in the second century, by a monastery dedicated to St. Peter and St. Paul, "which was the mother church and burial place to all Chester, and seven miles about Chester, and so continued for the space of three hundred years and more." To this monastery (according to Bradshaw the monk) the relics of Saint Werburgh, daughter of Wulphere, King of Mercia, were removed from Hanbury, in 875, for fear of an incursion of the Danes, and here re-buried with great pomp; a ceremony usually called "the translation of the body." The same author informs us that the army of Griffin, King of Wales, was stricken with blindness for their sacrilegious boldness, in attempting to disturb these sainted remains. This, and other reputed miracles of St. Werburgh, appear to have induced the celebrated Ethelfleda, Countess of Mercia, to translate the monastery of St. Peter and St. Paul, to the centre of the city, and to erect on its site a convent or monastery of secular nuns, dedicated to St. Werburgh and St. Oswald. Earl Leofric was a great benefactor to this foundation, having repaired its decayed buildings at his own expense : and in 1093, when (says Rodolphus Glaber) "princes strove *a vie* that cathedral churches and minsters should be erected in a more decent and seemly form, and when Christendom roused as it were herself, and, casting away her old habiliments, did put on every where the bright and white robe of the churches," Hugh Lupus expelled the canons secular, and laid the foundation of

a magnificent building, the remains of which are still existing ;
it was established by him as an Abbey of Benedictine Monks
from Bec in Normandy, to pray (as the foundation charter
expresses it) for the soul of William their King, and those of
King William his most noble father, his mother Queen Maud,
his brothers and sisters, King Edward the Confessor, themselves the founders, and those of their fathers, mothers, ante-
sessors, heirs, parents and barons, and of all christians as well
living as deceased." The confirmation charter by the second
Ranulf (surnamed De Gernon or Gernons), Earl of Chester,
in which the grant of Hugh Lupus is recapitulated, is in the
possession of the Marquis of Westminster, by whose kindness
this most important and interesting instrument has been lent for
the use of the Archæological Association, and has just been published in the pages of their journal. It is most beautifully written
in columns or pages, for the facility of reading. The charter
occupies nine, and commences with the copy of the original
grant of "Hugone Cestreasi comite, anno ab incarnatione
Domini milesimo nonugesimo" to the Abbey of St. Werburgh,
which was witnessed by Anselm, Archbishop of Canterbury,
followed by the grants of several of the other witnesses, and
it concludes by the confirmation of them all by the second
Ranulf : (Ego secundus Ranulfus comes Cæstrie concedo et
confirmo hos omnibus donationes quos mei antecessores vel ba-
rones eor'm dederunt,") with additional grants from himself.
Anselm, Abbot of Bec, afterward Archbishop of Canterbury,
regulated the new foundation and appointed Richard, his chaplain, the first abbot.

Hugh Lupus, following the example of most of his
predecessors, lived a life of the wildest luxury and rapine.
At length, falling sick from the consequence of his excesses,
and age and disease coming on, the old hardened soldier was
struck with remorse ; and—an expiation common enough in
those days—the great Hugh Lupus took the cowl, retired in
the last state of disease into the monastery, and in three
days was no more.

The Abbey was so richly endowed by the founder and his
successors, that at the dissolution, its revenues amounted to no
less a sum than £1,073 17s. 7d. per annum.

On the general dissolution of the monasteries, Chester was
erected into an independent bishoprick, and St. Werburgh's
was converted into a Cathedral Church, which it has ever
since remained. It was dedicated to Christ and the Blessed
Virgin Mary ; and a dean and six prebendaries installed in
it, Thomas Clarke, the last abbot, being appointed the first
dean.

The principal portions of this venerable pile have been erected at different periods from the fourteenth to the sixteenth century, although there are some parts which bear indubitable marks of a much earlier origin ; the greater part, perhaps, belong to the fourteenth or fifthteenth century, when the richly decorated style of Gothic architecture was at its zenith in this country. The Cathedral, from whatever side it is viewed, presents a massive appearance, and exhibits a pleasing variety of styles in accordance with the taste of different ages. Mr. Asphitel has said that he found beauties which grew on him more and more at every visit. The Norman remains are extremely fine—there is work of all kinds of great beauty— and there are the most curious and instructive transitions from style to style that perhaps were ever contained in one building.

Its general style may be termed the Norman-Gothic. It has been generally supposed that there are also some remaining specimens of the Saxon ; but Mr. Asphitel in an interesting lecture, delivered before the Archœlogical Association, stated that he could not, from the most minute research, discover any portion of the Saxon Church ; he considered it possible there might be some portions in the foundations, but none were visible.

The west front is said to have been the work of Abbot Ripley, who was appointed to the abbacy in 1485. It is now in an unfinished state, and it seems more than probable that there was an intention to form two western towers. The foundation of them was laid with much ceremony by Abbot Birchensaw in 1508, the Mayor being then present ; but the project was abandoned, most likely for want of funds ; had the original design been executed, says Winkle, it would not have been very imposing. The west entrance is a singular and beautiful composition ; the door itself is a Tudor arch, enclosed within a square head ; the spandrils are filled with rich and elegant foliations ; the hollow moulding on the top is deep and broad, and filled with a row of angels, half lengths ; all this is recessed within another Tudor arch, under another square head, with plain spandrils of ordinary pannelling. On each side of the door are four niches, with their usual accompaniments of crocketted canopies, pinnacles, and pendants ; and instead of brackets, the statues formerly stood on pedestals, with good bases and capitals. Above this entrance is the great western window of the nave, deeply and richly recessed ; it is of eight lights, with elaborate tracery of the kind most common in the latest age of the pointed style. The arch of the window is much depressed, and has above it a flowing crocketed canopy ; the gable has no parapet, but is finished off with a simple coping ; the flanking-turrets are octagonal, and have belts of pannelled tracery and embattled parapets. Leaving the west front, and turning to the south, a rich and deep porch presents itself behind the consistory court; the porch is flanked by buttresses, which once had pinnacles. The entrance is under a Tudor arch within a square head, the spandrils richly pannelled ; over the square head is a broad belt of quatre-foil pannelling ; above that a hollow moulding, adorned with the Tudor flower ; above this are two flat-headed windows of two lights each, with a deep niche between them, resting on a project-ing bracket, the statue is of course gone, but the projecting and richly decorated canopy remains, on both sides of which, the wall above is adorned with two rows of pannelling, the open embattled parapet which once crowned the whole has disappeared. The south side of the nave and its aisle is plain, but not without dignity ; the windows are all pointed and of perpendicular character, those of the aisle have straight canopies, with projecting buttresses between, which still have niches, and once had both pinnacles and statues ; the aisle has no parapet. The windows of the clerestory are unusually large and lofty, and their canopies are flowing in form, but perfectly plain and without finials, they have no buttresses between them, and the parapet is very shallow and quite plain.

The next feature of the Cathedral is a very singular one, and, indeed, unique, viz. the south wing of the transept. It is no uncommon case to find the two portions of the transept unlike each other in some respects ; but in no other instance are they so perfectly dissimilar as at Chester. Here the south wing is nearly as long as the nave, and of equal length with the choir, and considerably broader than either, having, like them, aisles on both sides ; while the north, which probably stands on the original foundations, has no aisles, is very short, and only just the breadth of one side of the central tower. The east and west faces of this south portion of the transept are nearly similar. The aisles have no parapet : the windows are pointed, of four lights each, with late decorated tracery and small intervening buttresses. The Clerestory has a parapet similar to that of the nave ; the windows are pointed, large, and lofty, with perpendicular tracery and two transoms. The south front of this transept, flat at top, is flanked with square embattled turrets and buttresses, and has a large window of the perpendicular age, filling up nearly all the space between them. The south face of the aisles on each side, have pointed windows and sloping tops, without parapet, but flanked by double buttresses at the external angles, without pinnacles.

The south face of the choir, with its aisle, is in nearly all respects similar to the south portion of the transept: but the aisle is lengthened out beyond the choir, and becomes the side aisle of the Lady Chapel, and has an octangular turret near the east end, with embattled parapet, and beyond it a plain heavy clumsy buttress; the sloping parapet of the east face of this aisle meets at the top the flat plain parapet of the most eastern compartment of the Lady Chapel which projects beyond the aisle, to that extent. The windows of the Lady Chapel are all pointed, and of good perpendicular character; the projecting portion has double buttresses at the external angles, and the eastern face has a low gable point. This chapel is very little higher than the side aisles of the choir, the east face of which is seen over it, with a large lofty pointed window, with perpendicular tracery and several transoms, flanked with octagonal turrets, engaged, and terminated with something like domes of Elizabethan architecture. The parapet of this east face of the choir is flat. The north side of Lady Chapel is similar to the south; the choir and its aisles exhibit features of an early English character on this side, but the Chapter-room conceals a considerable portion of it, which is a small building of an oblong form, and also of early English architecture. Over its vestibule and the arched passage leading into the east walk of the cloister, is seen the large window in the north front of the transept; the arch is much depressed, the tracery very common and plain, and it has two transoms; the walls of this wing of the transept are very plain, flat at top, and no parapet. The whole north side of the nave can be seen only from the cloister-yard. The south walk of the cloister is gone, and in the wall of the aisle, below the windows, are still seen several enriched semicircular arches resting on short cylindrical columns, evidently belonging to the original church of Hugh Lupus. The windows of the aisle are Tudor arched, with the ordinary tracery of this period; but, owing to the cloister once existing beneath, are necessarily curtailed of half their due length: there is a thin flat buttress between each; the aisle has no parapet. The clerestory is lofty, and the windows pointed, and not so much depressed as those in the aisle beneath: they are not so lofty as those in the south side, nor have they any canopies. There is a thin buttress between each, without pinnacles, and the parapet is quite plain, but not so shallow as that on the south side.

The central tower is perhaps the best external feature of

this Cathedral, it is indeed only of one story above the roof
ridge, but it is loftier than such towers usually are ; in each
face of it are two pointed windows, divided down the middle
with a single mullion, with a quatrefoil at the top, and all of
them having flowing crocketted canopies with finials. At each
of the four angles of the tower is an octagonal turret engaged,
all of which, like the tower itself, are terminated with an embattled parapet.

On entering the interior, through the west doorway into
the nave, "some disappointment and regret," says the same
authority, "cannot but be felt ; here is no vaulted roof, but
a flat ceiling of wood, resting on brackets of the same
material, slightly arched, which gives the nave the appearance
of having less elevation than it really possesses, for the naves
of many much more magnificent Cathedrals are not so lofty
as this by several feet, but by being vaulted their apparent
height is increased." The stone vaulting appears to have
been actually commenced, and was probably interrupted by
the dissolution ; it is to be regetted that the work was not
completed, as it would have given to the nave a much more
imposing effect. The north wall of the nave to the height
of the windows, is Norman work, and contains on the side
of the cloisters, six tombs, where, as it appears from an old
MS. written on the back of an old charter, now in the
British Museum, the early Norman Abbots are interred. Under
a wide arch sunk in the south wall, which from the ornaments
attached to the pillar near it, appears part of the original building, is a coffin-shaped stone with a cross fleury on the lid,
over the remains of some abbot. Nearly opposite to this, is
an altar tomb, the sides of which are ornamented with Gothic
niches, with trefoil heads, and with quatrefoils set alternately,
the quatrefoils being also alternately filled with roses and
leopards' heads ; the lid slides, and discloses the lead coffin,
a part of which has been cut away ; on the lid is a plain
coffin-shaped stone. It is highly probable that this tomb
contains the remains of one of the later abbots.

The pillars of the nave are clustered, and have rich
bases and foliated capitals, and the arches are pointed. In
this part of the Cathedral and the north transept, are
several monuments worthy the attention of visitors. A
pyramidical monument by Nollekins, representing a female
figure resting on a rock, against which is placed a broken
anchor ; erected by Capt. John Matthews, R.N. to the
memory of his wife. One, in white marble, by Banks,
representing the genius of history, weeping over an urn, having
three vols. inscribed "Longinus," "Thucydedes," "Zenophon,"

placed by it; erected to the memory of Dean Swift the
learned translator of those works.   One to the memory of
Mrs. Barbara Dod, erected by the minor canons.   One to Capt.
John William Buchanan, of the 16th light dragoons, slain at
the Battle of Warterloo.   One of Cavalier Sir Willm. Main-
waring, killed at Chester during the great civil war, 1644.
Against the north wall, a handsome monument, enclosing a
bust of Sir J. G. Egerton, Bart., erected by subscriptions of
the citizens of Chester, in memory of their honourable and
independent representative.   One in memory of Major Thos.
Hilton, who died at Montmeir, in the Burmese empire, 2nd
February, 1829. One to Augusta, the wife of the Revd. James
Slade, Canon of the Cathedral, and daughter of Bishop Law.
One of Capt. John Moor Napier, who died of asiatic cholera,
in Scinde, July 7th, 1846, aged 28 years: this monument was
executed by Westmacott, the inscription was written by his
uncle, the gallant Sir Charles Napier, and is as follows :—

> The tomb is no record of high lineage ;
> His may be traced by his name.
> His race was one of soldiers :
> Among soldiers he lived, among them he died,
> A soldier, falling where numbers fell with him
> In a barbarous land.
> Yet there died none more generous,
> More daring, more gifted, more religious.
> On his early grave
> Fell the tears of stern and hardy men,
> As his had fallen on the grave of others.

To the memory of their comrade, the officers of the General
Staff in Scinde erect this cenotaph.—[The above was executed
by Westmacott.]   In the north transept is a piece of very
fine tapestry, executed after one of the cartoons of Raphael,
representing the history of Elymas the sorcerer.   Wright, in
his travels through France and Italy, expresses his opinion
that this is much superior to any of the tapestry which he
saw in the Vatican.   There is also a well executed stone
monument to Roger Barnston, Esq. ; and a Tablet in memory
of good Chancellor Peploe.

The choir well merits the attention of every visitor of taste.
From the organ loft to the Bishop's throne, the sides are ornamented with rich spiral tabernacle work, underneath which are
massive and highly ornamented stalls.   The choir is separated
from the nave and broad aisle by a Gothic stone screen ; there
are five pointed arches on each side; above them, is an arcade
of pointed arches, resting on slender shafts, and above it are

the clerestory windows. The pavement of the choir is of
black and white marble. At the west end of it, are four stalls
on each side of the entrance, and there are twenty others on
each side of the choir; over these are rich canopies, with
pinnacles and pendants in great profusion. Above the stalls
on the right hand, opposite the pulpit, is the Bishop's throne,
which formerly stood at the east end in St. Mary's Chapel,
and is said to have been the shrine of St. Werburgh, or as
suggested by Pennant, the pedestal on which originally
stood the real shrine which contained the sacred reliques. At
the Reformation it was removed to its present position, and converted into a throne for the Bishop. It is a rich specimen of
Gothic architecture, decorated with carved work, and embellished
with a range of thirty curious small statues, variously habited, holding scrolls in their hands, and originally inscribed
with their names, but now defaced. Dr. Cowper published in
1799, an elaborate history of these figures, and was of opinion
that they represented kings and saints of the royal Mercian line,
ancestors or relations of St. Werburgh. Very great improvements
have recently been effected within the choir. The restoration
of the bishop's throne was effected by the munificence of the
Rev. Canon Slade, as an obituary testimonial to his late father-
in-law, Bishop Law, in memory of whom, the following inscription, engraven upon a brass plate, is affixed to the throne:—

In gloriam Dei hanc cathedram reficiendam curabit A.D. MDCCCXLVI.
Jacobus Slade, A.M, hujus ecclesiae Canonicus. Necnon in piam me-
moriam Georgii Henrici Law, S.T.P. per xii. annos Episcopi Cestriensis,
dein Bathoniensis.

At the back of the throne is a magnificent stone screen, the
gift of the Archbishop of Canterbury. The altar screen was presented by the Rev. Peploe Hamilton, of Hoole, near Chester;
the chair within the communion table by the Rev. Canon Blomfield; the new bible desk, of carved oak in the form of an eagle,
by the Rev. Chancellor Raikes; the new stone pulpit, from a
beautiful design by Mr. Massey, is the liberal gift of Sir Edwd.
S. Walker, of this city. Towards the restoration of the cathedral, Her Majesty the Queen also contributed a donation of £105
in the name of the Prince of Wales as Earl of Chester.

Under the east window is an arch opening to the Lady Chapel,
which consists of a middle and two side aisles, the stone vaulting
of which is adorned with richly carved key-stones. The side
aisles are divided from the middle portion of two arches, sprung
from a massy pier on each side, apparently part of the original
building, cut down and crusted over with clusters of light pillars,
terminated in elegant pointed arches, with quatrefoils inserted

in the mouldings.   On the north side of the chancel, which
extends beyond the side aisles, are two elegant pointed arches;
one contains two piscinas; the other was apparently a seat for
the officiating priest; another pointed arch appears also on the
opposite side.

The cloisters are on the north side of the Church, and form
a quadrangle of 110 feet square.   Originally these were four
walks, but the south walk is destroyed.   The general style of
the cloisters is that of the fifteenth century, with carved cornice
key-stones at the intersections of the vaulting; the arches of
the windows are depressed.   A lavatory projects from the
west walk of the cloisters, and did extend along the south
walk ; over the east walk was a dormatory, which was some
time ago destroyed, much to the injury of the appearance of
these venerable conventual ruins.   It is obvious that the
present cloisters are only a restoration of an earlier one.   In
the east walk of the cloisters is the entrance into the Chapter
House.   The stone vaulting rests in clusters of slender shafts,
with foliated capitals ; notwithstanding the soft nature of the
stone, the carving is all in a good state of preservation.   The
chapter house was built in the beginning of the twelfth
century, by Randle, Earl of Chester, who removed hither
from the churchyard, the body of his uncle Hugh Lupus,
whose remains were found enclosed in a stone coffin in 1723,
by persons employed in digging in the chapter house.   The
scull and bones were entire, and lay in their proper position,
enveloped in an ox-hide.   On the breast was a piece of cloth,
the texture of which could not be ascertained.   Mr. Asphitel
considers the chapter house, with its singularly tasteful vestibule, to be the finest in the kingdom.

We now direct the visitor's attention to a portion of the
Norman edifice, which has of late excited very great interest,
the Promptuarium, lately excavated; "the chamber is a sort of
gallery or cloister on the ground floor, about ninety feet long
by forty feet wide, traversed in the centre by a row of pillars
(with one exception cylindrical), which divide it into six
double bays, from which pillars, and four corresponding ones
at each side, spring the intersecting arches by which the
building is vaulted.   The side pillars are as entirely Norman
in their character as the centre ones, being simply the square
pier, on each face of which is the pilaster attached ; the
groining of the roof is without the finish of ribs at the joints,
a finish characteristic of a later period.   The chamber, which
has at present only a borrowed light from the cloisters on the
east, was originally lighted from the west side, by a window
in each bay, except the second bay from the south end, in

which was a principal entrance. This doorway and the windows are now all choked up by the adjoining garden. On the same side, and at the north end, is a very large chimney and fire-place. A glance at the groining and arches at the north end informing us that the chamber did formerly end here, I was induced to think, by this situation of the fire-place, that its length was originally very much greater. I have since found the termination of the chamber in the cellars of the present Registry, where the groining is supported by corbels, which shew that the vaults extended there, but no further. One double bay, therefore, added to the present remains, gives us the entire length of the building,—about one hundred and five feet. In this last bay, on the east side, is a principal doorway (four inches wider than the one on the west side), leading towards the Refectory. On the east side also, and near the north end, is a postern from the cloisters and a spiral staircase, partly constructed in the thickness of the wall, leading to the chamber above, of which there are now no remains. Two small archways at opposite sides of the chamber, precisely similar in form and size, and rising from beneath the level of the floor, seemed to indicate a subterranean passage connecting them. An excavation round each has, however, discovered no channel between them. In considering the character and situation of this vaulted chamber it should be borne in mind that though now apparently sub-terranean, it is only so with reference to the west side, the level of the floor being four feet above the level of the nave of the Cathedral. The ground which now rises above it on the west side is all *made* ground of late date, belonging to the Palace, the original level of which is identical with this chamber, as shewn by the area round the present Palace kitchens, and by those apartments belonging to the Abbot's residence, which yet remain."*

Mr Asphitel, in his able lecture on Chester Cathedral, bestowed the name of Promptuarium on this Norman cloister, he says, "these are vaulted apartments of early Norman work, and are described in the charter of Henry 8th, by which he divides the properties between the bishop and dean, *promptuaria et pannaria*, the former derived from a word devoting a butler or steward, probably a buttery ; and the latter, from *pannus*, a cloth, probably the place for clothing."

Mr. Ayrton, in an able paper on the Norman remains of the Cathedral, read before the Chester Archæological Association, entered into an elaborate enquiry on the subject, stating his

* Mr. W. Ayrton on the Norman remains of the Cathedral.

reasons for concluding that this is not a *Promptuarium*, but, in his opinion, a spacious Hall, where the splendid hospitality of the Abbots was displayed to strangers, friends, and dependents.*

There is a vaulted passage at the south end of the *Promptuarium*, leading from the Abbot's apartments to the Cathedral; the arches are circular, the groining is ribbed with elliptical mouldings, these mouldings stamp a semi-Norman character on the work, being almost a transition to the early English style.

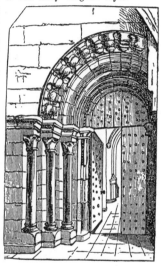

NORMAN DOORWAY.

"Two beautiful Norman doorways gave ingress and egress from the passage, and still remain, though the one which opened to the present west cloister is closed, and sadly disfigured by the alterations of the sixteenth century. The other doorway to the west is yet perfect, excepting the shafts of the pillars which are gone. At the south end of the east cloister, and forming the present entrance from that cloister to the Cathedral, is a Norman doorway of about the same date as the arcade adjoining it. The architrave is very ornate, bearing the billet ornaments, accompanied by a bead which runs between the mouldings; the capitals of the pilasters are foliated, and identical with those already noticed in the Norman doorway of the vaulted passage."

The dimensions of the Cathedral are as follows:—Length from east to west, 350 feet; nave, 160; choir, 125; Lady Chapel, 65; transept from north to south, 180; breadth of nave, choir, and aisles, $74\frac{1}{2}$ feet; south wing of transept, 80 feet square; height of nave and choir, 78 feet; tower, 127; Lady Chapel, 33; north wing of transept, 39 feet broad.

* The reader is referred to a History of the Cathedral, by J. Bayne, to be had of the publisher of this work, in which Mr. Ayrton's able and interesting arguments are given at length.

The following is a list of the bishops from the foundation of
the see in 1541 to the present date :—

John Bird	1541	Thomas Cartwright	1688
George Cotes	1554	Nicholas Stratford	1689
Cuthbert Scott	1555	William Dawes	1707
William Downham	1561	Francis Gastrell	1714
William Chadderton	1579	Samuel Peploe	1716
Hugh Bellot	1595	Edmund Keene	1752
Richard Vaughan	1597	William Markham	1771
George Lloyd	1604	Beilby Porteus	1777
Gerard Massie	1615	William Cleaver	1788
Thomas Moreton	1616	H. W. Majendie	1800
John Bridgeman	1618	E. B. Sparke	1810
Brian Walton	1660	G. H. Law	1812
Henry Ferne	1662	C. J. Blomfield	1824
George Hall	1662	J. B. Sumner	1828
John Wilkins	1668	J. Graham	1848
John Pearson	1672		

List of Deans of Chester Cathedral, from its formation to
the present time.

Thomas Clarke	1541	James Arderne	1682
Henry Mann	1542	Lawrence Fogg	1691
William Cliff	1547	Walter Offley	1718
Richard Walker	1558	Thomas Allen	1721
John Pears	1567	Thomas Brooke	1733
R. Langworth	1571	William Smith	1758
R. Dorset	1579	George Cotton	1780
Thomas Modesley	1580	Hugh Cholmondeley	1806
John Rutter	1589	Robert Hodgson	1815
Wm. Barlow	1602	Peter Vaughan	1820
Henry Parry	1605	Edmund Copleston	1826
Thomas Mallory	1607	Henry Philpotts	1828
Wm. Nicholls	1644	George Davys	1830
Henry Bridgman	1660	F. Anson	1839

BISHOP—J. Graham, D. D.   DEAN—F. Anson, D. D.

ARCHDEACONS.

Ven. Isaac Wood, Middlewich | Ven. J. Brooks, Liverpool

CANONS.

Rev. J. Slade, M.A.   Rev. T. Eaton, M.A.
Rev. G. B. Blomfield, M.A.   Rev. Temple Hillyard, M.A.

MINOR CANONS.

R. W. Gleadowe, M.A.   W. H. Massie, M.A.
W. Harrison, M.A.   F. E. Thurland, B.A., Precentor, &c.

HONORARY CANONS.

Rev. Henry Raikes, M.A.   Rev. Hugh McNeile, D.D.
Rev. C. A. Thurlow, M.A.   Rev. Hugh Stowell, M.A.

Organist—Mr. Gunton.

The service of the Cathedral is performed with great solemnity and fine taste; and the talented organist, Mr. Gunton, merits great praise for the admirable manner in which he fulfils his duties.

The hours of Service are:—Week-day: morning 7 10; afternoon, 4. Sunday: morning, 11; afternoon, 4 o'clock. During the winter months the service begins at 3 in the afternoon. There is an anthem every day in the afternoon service.

Through the indefatigable energy of Dr. Anson, the present Dean, many most important improvements have been introduced into the interior of this noble edifice, which have added very much to its decoration and general effect. In 1843, the munificent sum of £4000 was contributed for the purpose of giving effect to the praiseworthy object of restoring some portion of the ancient beauties of the Cathedral. A new organ has been erected, of great power and richness of tone, the top of which is carved with tabernacle work, in unison with that of the choir. The old pews, which were sadly out of keeping with the rich Gothic woodwork of the stalls, have been removed, and the choir has been new seated in the Gothic style.

The whole of the choir has been vaulted, which has greatly contributed to its improved appearance. Three beautiful stained glass windows have been placed at the east end of the choir and the Lady Chapel, which have given a much more solemn and impressive aspect to the interior. The clerestory window of the choir has five figures, representing our Saviour and the four Evangelists, surrounded with their various emblems; over which are five scenes from the life of Christ, viz., the Agony in the Garden; Bearing the Cross; the Crucifixion; the Resurrection; and the Ascension. This window was executed by Mr. Wailes, of Newcastle-under-Lyne, at the cost of £200. The window of the Lady Chapel represents, in its lower divisions, the following important transactions in the history of the Redeemer's sojourn upon earth:—The Annunciation to the Shepherds—the Nativity—the Offerings of

the Wise Men of the East—the Presentation in the Temple—
Christ Disputing with the Doctors—the Baptism—the Miracle
of turning the Water into Wine—Healing the Lame—Walking
on the Sea—Feeding the Multitude—the Transfiguration—the
Raising of Lazarus—the Entry into Jerusalem—Washing the
Desciples' Feet—and the Last Supper.   The upper division of
the window contains figures of the twelve Apostles ; ranged in
the order in which their names are given in Sacred Writ.
This window was also executed by Mr. Wailes, at the cost
of £360, and of the outer guards £60.

A magnificent window by the same artist, has also been
placed in the south aisle of the choir, by the Very Rev. the
Dean, in memory of three deceased members of his family.
The inscription is as follows :—

"Sancta Catherina—'The souls of the righteous are in the
hand of God.'—Catherine Louisa Anson, died and buried at
Southwell, March 28, 1832, aged 18, 3rd daughter."

"Sanctus Thomas—'Thy brother shall rise again'—Thomas
Anson, Lieut. R. N., died and buried at Sudbury, March 17,
1845, aged 24, 4th son."

"Sancta Maria—'The Lord gave and the Lord hath taken
away.'—Mary Blomfield, wife of the Rev. G. B. Blomfield,
Canon of Chester, died and buried at Stevenage, August 6,
1848, aged 38, 2nd daughter of the Rev. Frederick Anson,
D.D., Dean of Chester, by whom this memorial is placed."

Another obituary window has more recently been erected,
placed next to the latter.   It is in memory of George Edwd.
Anson, Esq., son of the Dean of Chester.   The inscription is
as follows:—In memory of George Edwd. Anson, Esq. C.B.,
Keeper of H. M. Privy Purse ; Treasurer of H. R. H. Prince
Albert, and to the Prince of Wales.   Suddenly called away
from the faithful but unostentatious discharge of high official
duties to his rest in Christ, on the 9th day of October, 1849,
aged 37.   He was the 2nd son of the Rev. Frederick Anson,
D. D., Dean of this Cathedral, with whose bereavement the
inhabitants of this city and neighbourhood record their sympathy, and commemorate his zeal in the restoration of the
Cathedral Church, by erecting this memorial window.   Mr.
Hardman of Birmingham was the artist, and the cost of the
window £180.   The events represented are the raising of Jairus'
Daughter—Raising of Lazarus—Raising the Widow's Son—En-
tombment and Resurrection of our Lord—and our Lord appearing
to Mary.

CHURCH OF ST. OSWALD'S,

As already mentioned, forms the south transept of the choir
of Chester Cathedral.   After the introduction of regular monks

into the monastery of St. Werburgh, anciently dedicated to the Holy Trinity and St. Oswald, the name of this patron Saint was retained by that part of the conventual church which was set apart for the uses of the inhabitants of the parish, within which the monastery was placed. This part probably occupied the site of that transept of the Cathedral which forms the present parish church. The name of St. Oswald does not, however, appear to have been originally used for the parish. In the license of appropriation by William Cornhall, Bishop of Coventry, it is called the parish church of St. Werburgh.

It appears to have been subsequently called the church of Saint Oswald and the Church of Saint Werburgh indiscriminately. It was founded in the ninth century by Ethelfleda, Countess of Mercia. So early as 1093, when Earl Leofric introduced regular monks into the Cathedral, that part of it now occupied by St. Oswald's was set apart for the use of the parishioners as we have just stated. The abbot and convent afterwards wishing to re-attach it to the Cathedral, built for the parishioners a small chapel, dedicated to St. Nicholas, in the spot where the Theatre now stands; but they do not appear to have been contented with their new place of worship, for in 1488, we find from 'Gastrel's Notitia,' that a "composition was made between the abbot and the parishioners of St. Oswald's for their new church." They accordingly re-entered into the south transept, which had been rebuilt by Abbot Ripley, and have ever since used it as their parish church. In 1525 there were no seats in this church, except those appropriated to the mayor and corporation, who at that period regularly attended this place of worship.

Bishop Bridgeman seems to have wished to re-unite St. Oswald's to the Cathedral, and with this intention attempted to transfer parochial service to the broad aisle; preparations were made; a pulpit was provided, and the rector was directed to preach in this part of the Cathedral. The project was regarded with great disapprobation by the parishioners, who refused to attend in any other place than their own church, and the Bishop therefore was obliged to give up his intention. St. Oswald's was formerly in a state of great delapidation; and was only separated from the aisle of the Cathedral by a slight wooden screen. In 1827 it was thoroughly repaired; the whole was new flagged and pewed, a new pulpit and reading desk added; the old gallery, which was at the west side, taken down, and a new one erected at the south end. The interior was cut off from the aisle by a partition, erected by Dr. Copplestone, at his own expense; this worthy and munificent Dean carried out also many other most important improvements in

G

the Cathedral. The exterior of the south aisle of the choir he refaced with freestone, and erected a beautiful octagonal tower at its eastern extremity, besides cutting away and removing the surface soil, which had accumulated to the height of several feet round the walls of the choir and St. Mary's Chapel. The repairs of St. Oswald's and the Cathedral cost the Dean upwards of £1000.

St. Oswald's is now a most commodious and handsome place of worship; it is a vicarage in the gift of the Dean and Chapter of Chester Cathedral. The present vicar is the Rev. William Harrison, M.A.

CHURCH OF ST. JOHN THE BAPTIST.

The church is situated without the city walls, a short distance from the Newgate; it stands upon an elevation overhanging the north bank of the Dee, and the churchyard commands a beautiful and extensive prospect.

This church, with its adjoining ruins, is the most interesting of the ecclesiastical buildings of the city. When we take into consideration its venerable antiquity, and the significant mutations by which its history is distinguished, we may venture to say that it is one of the oldest and most interesting ecclesiastical foundations now extant in Britain. The specimens of early architecture, and the curious monumental remains the church contains, render it eminently deserving the investigation of the antiquarian, while the historic events connected with it, will doubtless afford interest to all.

The foundation of the church is ascribed by Webb to Ethelred, king of Mercia, and stated on the authority of Giraldus, to have taken place in the year 689. The MSS. chronicle of St. Werburgh makes a similar statement on the same authority; it is also adopted by the author of Polycronicon, and thus quaintly recorded—

" The year of grace six hundred fourscore nine,
So saith my author, a Briton, Giraldus,
King Etheldred, minding most the bliss of heaven,
Edified a college church, notable and famous,
In the suburbs of Chester, pleasant and beauteous,
In the honour of God, and the Baptist St. John,
With the help of Bishop Wulfrice, and good exhortation."

This inscription is now affixed to a pillar on the north side of the church. With respect to its foundation by Ethelred, we find the following curious passage, quoted from an early writer by King and others :—" King Ethelred minding to build a church, was told that when he should see a white hind there he should build a church, which white hind he saw in the place where St. John's church now standeth, and in remembrance whereof, his picture was placed in the wall of the said church, which yet standeth on the side of the steeple, towards the west, having a white hind in his hand."

According to William of Malmsbury, St. John's was repaired and richly endowed by Leofric, Earl of Mercia, in 1057, and it is shortly afterwards thus noticed in Doomsday Book:—"Ecclesia Sancti Johanius, in civitale habét viii. domos, quietas ab omné consuetudine: una ex his est matricularii ecclesiæ ; aliæ sunt canonicorum." The seat of the See, which for some centuries after the conquest fluctuated between Chester, Coventry, and Lichfield, was in 1075, fixed for a time in the church of St. John, by Peter, then bishop, which may be taken as a sufficient proof of the wealth and grandeur of the foundation, even at this early period. The succeeding bishop, Robert de Limesey, having removed the seat of the See to Coventry, St. John's returned to its former collegiate establishment, but was long afterwards considered and denominated one of the three Cathedrals of the diocese, and retained in its immediate neighbourhood a palace of the bishop, and the mansion of the archdeacon of Chester—the remains of its former importance. At the dissolution in 1547, the college consisted of one dean, seven prebends, four vicars, a clerk, and a sexton. " In this church," says Dr. Cowper, "was an ancient rood or image of wood of such veneration, that in a deed dated March 27, 1311, confirmed by Walter Langton, the church was called the *Church of the Holy Cross and St. John.*" "There can be little doubt on the whole," says Ormerod, "that some monastic foundation dedicated to the holy cross, had, previously to this, merged in the college of St. John." In 1468, the old steeple, which stood between the nave and the chancel, fell in and destroyed great part of the choir. In 1470, the steeple was rebuilt, and the whole church covered with lead at the expense of the parishioners, to whom certain immunities were granted by the Dean on that account. In 1548, a commision was granted to certain gentlemen of Cheshire to survey the colleges, &c. within the county, in virtue whereof a return (now in the Augmentation Office) was made, wherein the annual rent of the college of St. John, arising from lands, tithes. &c. is reckoned at £146. 5s. The church plate is estimated in the same return at 465 ounces; the weight of the five bells 4000lbs.; lead in and upon the church 78 tons; and goods and ornaments for the use of the clergy to the value of £40. 19s. 9d. In 1572, the greater part of the central steeple again fell in; and in 1574, part of the steeple at the west end of the church also gave way, whereby great part of the church was destroyed.

After being suffered to remain in a ruinous state for some years, the parishioners obtained a grant of the church from Queen Elizabeth in 1581, whereupon they repaired and reduced it to its present size and form, by taking down the remains of the central steeple, and cutting off the south and north transepts and all the chapels above the choir. In 1585, the Queen granted the impropriate rectory and advowson to Sir Christopher Halton, by whom it was conveyed to Alexander King, who in 1587, conveyed it to Alexander Cotes, whose daughter brought it by marriage to the family of the Sparkes in 1597, in which family it continued until the year 1810, when it was sold by their representative John Adams, Esq. to the late Marquis of Westminister, who in 1813 rebuilt the north and south transepts and repaired the chancel, in which he introduced a Gothic window over the altar.

"St. John's when entire," says Pennant, "was a magnificent pile. The tower once stood in the centre, but falling down in 1574 was never rebuilt." "The church," says Ormerod, "was in the finest style of early Norman Architecture; it consisted originally of a nave and choir, with side aisles, two transepts and a central tower, &c."

On each side of the chancel were added at a later period, chapels in a rich style of pointed Gothic, in which some exquisite specimens of shrine work are yet remaining. It remains now to speak of the present appearance of these venerable ruins.

The nave and choir, fitted up and repaired in 1581, as before mentioned, now form the parish church in which public worship is celebrated. Eight arches resting on pillars 5 feet 6 inches in circumference, with capitals variously ornamented, separate the nave from the side aisles, and above these are two rows of galleries with pointed arches springing from light shafts. Four massive composite pillars, which formerly supported the central tower, still remain in the nave. In the interior are some interesting relics of the architecture of our Saxon ancestors, combined with that of their Norman-English successors.

The belfry is detached from the church, at the north-west corner of which it is situate. It is a square tower erected in the seventeenth century, 150 feet in height. It is extremely lofty, and its sides are decorated with pointed windows in a good style, figures placed in rich shrines, strings of quatrefoils and rows of ornamental arches; in one of the niches on the west side is placed the "picture" of King Ethelred before described, removed thither at the erection of the new tower, from amongst the rubbish in which it had lain since the fall of the central tower in which it formerly stood. It is much defaced by time and exposure to the weather.

At the east end of the church, as now rebuilt, stand the ruins of the chapels above the choir, consisting of the outer walls, with the remains of several windows of Gothic architecture, and the eastern wall containing a beautiful arched window of the same style, but larger and richer in ornament than the others.

Near the foot of the tower, on the north side of the church, is an ancient porch, forming the principal entrance, in the sides of which are two lancet arches, the entrance being under an acutely pointed arch, the mouldings of which rest on a number of short shafts, which converge as they retire inwards.

"Within this church," says Ormerod, "was a chantry, dedicated to St. Mary." Within the precincts of St. John's were also Thorneton's chantry, the chapel of St. Anne, which Pigott says, in some deeds, is called the '*Monastery* of St. Anne;' it was endowed with land and houses, some of which now constitute the revenues of Northwich school;" there was also the chapel of St. James's, which Lyson says, was the old parish church; in 1662 it is described as being then used as a stable. It has long since been entirely destroyed. On the south wall of the churchyard was an ancient building, called the "Anchorite's Cell," which is said to be the spot where Earl Harold retired after the battle of Hastings in 1066. In 1770 two skeletons were discovered here in coffin-shaped cavities, scooped out of the rock. The fourteen panel tablets which are hung in various parts of the church, bearing the arms of the deceased to whose memory they are placed, are said to be painted by one of the Randle Holmes, the distinguished herald artists. The modern Gothic gallery on the north side of the chancel was erected by the late Marquis of Westminster, for the use of the children educated at his public school, which is situate close by. A new organ has been erected, purchased with a sum of money left for that purpose by the late rector, the Rev. William Richardson. The present vicar is the Rev. W. B. Marsden, M.A.

St. Peter's Church.

This church stands exactly in the centre of the city, where the four principal streets meet, and close to the ancient site of the high cross. It consists of a nave and side aisles, divided from each other by three pointed arches. The span of the arches, and the height of the building," says Ormerod, "are very disproportionate to the present size of the interior, and gives it the appearance of being a fragment of a much larger building." In a square tower on the south-west side are eight bells, cast in 1709, whereof six are a peal; on the treble is engraved, "When you ring, I'll sing."

The pentice bell was cast in 1589, and was formerly used for summoning the magistrates to their duties. The interior of the church is handsomely and commodiously pewed.

Pennant is of opinion, as we have before stated, that on this site formerly stood the Roman Prœtorium. Tradition says that this church was built by Ethelfleda, Countess of Mercia, and that it was originally dedicated to St. Peter and St. Paul, at the time when the name of the "mother church" was changed to the Holy Trinity and St. Oswald. Bradshaw, the Monk, alluding thereto says—

> And the old church of St. Peter and Paul,
> By a general consent of the spirituality,
> With the help of the Duke most principal,
> Was translated into the midst of the said city.

In Domesday it is noticed under its present name, "templum Sancti Petri;" and it is there stated "nunquam pertinuet ad manerium extra civitatem, sed ad burgum pertinet, et semper fuit in consuetudine regis et comitis, sicut aliorum burgensium." In 1081, it was given by Robert de Rodeland to the Monks of St. Ebrulf in Normandy, by whom it was shortly afterwards resigned to the Abbot of St. Werburgh. In 1479, the steeple was rebuilt, on which occasion the parson and other inhabitants ate a goose on the top of it, and flung the bones into the four principal streets beneath. In 1580, eight yards of the spire of the steeple were new built. A.D. 1637-40, the east end of the church, and the south side from the window stools, was re-edificed, the roof almost new leaded, most of the pews new made, all the rest repaired, and all the aisles flagged. At the dissolution the patronage of St. Peter's was vested in the Dean and Chapter of Chester; it afterwards reverted to the Crown, but is now solely in the gift of the Bishop. The spire of this church having been injured by lightning, was taken down in 1780, and in 1787 the south side of the church was re-cased with stone. The steeple was rebuilt and a new clock was placed in it in 1813. The present rector is the Rev. F. Ford, M.A.

Sunday evening lectures were established in this church in 1818, under the patronage of Bishop Law. These are supported by annual subscriptions aided by collections at the church. The present lecturer is the Rev. Wm. Clarke, B.D. incumbent of Little St. John's.

THE CHURCH OF THE HOLY TRINITY

Is situated on the north side of Watergate-street, adjoining the Custom House.

All traces of the foundation and endowment of this church

are buried in remote antiquity. The earliest evidence of its existence now to be found is in a charter relative to the church of Rosthern, in the twelfth century, amongst the witnesses to which is "Walterus Ecclesiæ Sanctæ Trinitatis Presbyterus." The advowson was anciently vested in the Barons of Montalt now called Hawarden, with which barony it passed to the Crown, by whom it was given to the Earls of Salisbury, from whom it passed to the Stanleys of Lathom, whose representative, the Earl of Derby, is the present patron. In 1401, Henry Prince of Wales and Earl of Chester (afterwards Henry the Fifth), confirmed to the citizens of Chester a charter, whereby they were relieved from payment of tithes for the Roodeye to the Parson of Trinity parish. In 1679, the south and east sides of this church being in a ruinous state, were rebuilt. The tower was formerly surmounted by a remarkably light and elegant spire 159 feet in height. This, however, from the perishable nature of its materials and its exposed situation, required very frequent repairs, and about seventy-five years ago the upper part was so frequently and severely injured by storms, as to require rebuilding thrice in eight years. In 1811, the whole structure of the spire was in such a state of decay, that reasonable doubts were entertained of its safety, if allowed to remain; it was therefore taken down and the tower reduced to its present altitude. The burying ground adjoining this church having been found inadequate to the increased population of the parish, a piece of ground to the eastward of the city gaol was purchased in 1809, and converted to that purpose, at an expense of £1000.

The interior of this church consists of a nave, chancel, and side aisles, divided from the nave by three pointed arches on the south side; but on the north the arches have been removed, and their places supplied by iron pillars. A thorough repair took place in 1826, when a number of free sittings were erected in the galleries.

Dr. Parnell, archdeacon of Clogher, whose poems are familiar to every person of taste and feeling, was buried in this church, October 24th, 1718, having died at Chester on his way to Ireland.

There are several monuments in this church worthy of attention. Within the communion rails lie the remains of Matthew Henry, the celebrated commentator, who officiated in the Presbyterian chapel, in Crook-street; there is a Latin inscription to his memory on a brass plate, which runs thus :—
" Matthew Henry, pietatis et ministerii officiis strenue perfunctus per labores, S.S. literis scrutandiset explicandis impenso, cenfectum carpus huic dormitorio commiset 22 die Junii, 1714. Anno ætat. 52."

St. Martin's Church,

Formerly called *St. Martin's of the Ash*, stands at the west end
of White Friars and Cuppin-street. It appears to have been
an ancient foundation; for it is mentioned in a deed, in the
year 1250, wherein Bernard de Trannuille releases to Philip le
Clerk a rent of 12d. arising from premises situate "near the
church of St. Martin in Chester." The old church mentioned
in this deed, having fallen into decay, was rebuilt in 1721, as
we learn from an inscription on the front of the steeple. It
is a remarkably small but very neat structure, pointed with
stone at the angles and finishings. The interior is handsomely
fitted up. The open ground in front of this church bears the
name of *Martin's Ash*, derived in all likelihood from the circumstance of an ash tree having formerly stood on the spot.
The parish is now united to that of St. Bridget, and the
service in the church is discontinued.

St. Mary's Church,

Anciently called *Ecclesia Sanctœ Mariœ de Castello* and *Ecclesia
Sanctœ Mariœ super Montem,* but now *St. Mary's on the Hill*,
stands at the upper end of Castle-street, at the extreme verge
of the liberties of the city.

Although the precise date of the foundation of this church
cannot now be ascertained, yet it is not improbable that it
was one of those founded early in the twelfth century by
Lucy, sister of Edwin, Earl of Mercia, and widow of Randle
de Meschines, Earl of Chester, a lady remarkable as a bene-
factress to the "holy church," even in that church-erecting
and endowing age. At all events, St. Mary's was gifted to
the abbey of St. Werburgh, by Randle Gernons, Earl of
Chester, son of the above named lady, in one of those fits of
compunction which usually followed the acts of violence into
which his turbulence and ambition frequently led him. Shortly
after the dissolution, the Dean and Chapter of St. Werburgh
obtained a grant from the Crown of the rectory of St. Mary's,
which was surrendered by Dean Cliffe in 1550, to Sir R. Cotton,
in the manner described in a former part of this work,
by whose agent it was sold for £100 to John Brereton,
Esq. of Wettenhall, by whose heirs it was again sold to the
Wilbrahams of Dorfold, from whom it passed by marriage to
the Hills of Hough, in Wybunbury, from whom it was purchased by the late Marquis of Westminster.

St. Mary's consists of a nave, chancel, and side aisles, with
a square tower at the west end, used as a belfry. The south
aisle, called *Troutbeck's Chapel*, was erected by William Troutbeck, of Dunham, in the fifteenth century. This chapel is

noticed in the ecclesiastical survey taken by the Commissioners appointed by Henry the Eighth, and its annual rents, arising from lands and tenements within the city of Chester, are estimated at £5. 6s. In this chapel were many monuments of the founder's family, which, according to Holmes, "were thought to exceed any thing of the kind in England," but these were destroyed by the falling in of the roof in 1660. In 1690, the parishioners having obtained a grant of the site from the Duke of Shrewsbury, representative of the Troutbecks, built thereon the present south aisle. The north aisle was anciently called the *Chapel of St. Catherine.*

The tower of St. Mary's is only 50 feet high, its further elevation having been objected to by the Governor of Chester castle, when it was repaired in 1715, lest it should command the castle-yard.

The interior of this church is neatly fitted up with commodious and handsome pews. In 1793, an organ was put up in the west gallery by Mr. Chalinor. A beautiful window of stained glass has recently been introduced, which has very much improved the interior.

In this church are several monuments well worthy the attention of the visitor. Amongst these is one to the memory of Thos. Gamul, Recorder of Chester, who died in 1613. The deceased is represented in a recumbent posture, with his wife on his right hand, and his only son in the attitude of prayer at his knee : on the side of the tomb his three daughters who died in infancy, holding skeletons in their hands. The statues of this monument are of alabaster. Another to the memory of Philip Oldfield, of Bradwell, who died in 1616, represents him in the costume of that age, leaning on his right side, with a roll of parchment in his hand. The slab is supported by kneeling figures of his four sons, with their hands upon their sword hilts : at the head are figures of his two daughters bearing shields. In the north aisle are tablets to the memory of different members of the family of Holmes, the celebrated antiquaries. Of this family, four successively bore the name of Randle. The first, who was Sheriff of Chester in 1615, and Mayor in 1633, died in 1654 ; the second was Mayor of Chester in 1643, and died in 1659 ; the third, author of the "Academic Armoury," was gentleman sewer to Charles the Second, and Deputy Garter King of Arms, and died in 1699 ; and the fourth was Deputy Norroy King of Arms, and died in 1707. Of these four Randle Holmes' the second and third were the celebrated antiquarian collectors, and there are some compilations of a similar nature brought down to 1704 by the last.

St. Mary's is a rectory in the gift of the Marquis of Westminster. The present rector is the Rev. W. H. Massie, M.A.

There are Sunday evening lectures in this church, under the
patronage of the Bishop of the Diocese. They are supported
by annual subscriptions, aided by collections in the church.
The present lecturer is the Rev. W. P. Hutton, M.A.

ST. BRIDGET'S CHURCH.

The old church of St. Bridget or St. Bride (now removed),
was situate on the west side of Bridge-street, exactly opposite
to St. Michael's. There exist no correct data on which to ascertain the time of its foundation, which tradition attributes to
Offa, King of Mercia, who reigned in the end of the eighth
century, about which time we are told that several churches
were founded in Chester. There is, however, clear evidence
from writings among the Harleian MSS. that in the twelfth
century the patronage of this church belonged to the Lords of
Aldford, by one of whom, in 1224, it was quitclaimed to Randle
Blundeville. From another writing it appears that, in 1265,
Simon, Abbot of St. Werburgh, in consideration of certain
grants and donations, made to him by Bertram de Arneway,
bound himself to maintain a chaplain to say mass for the soul
of John Arneway, before the altar of the virgin in St. Bridget's
church. This church was formerly surrounded by a wall which
encroached considerably upon Bridge-street, and the ground between this wall and the church was used as a burying place;
but in 1785 the bodies were removed to a piece of ground on
the south of the church, and the street widened. The church
walls were refaced with freestone and other repairs made at
the same time. A gateway formerly crossed the street between
St. Bridget's and St. Michael's churches, dividing higher from
lower Bridge-street. The old church of St. Bridget was taken
down in 1827, under the provisions of the New Bridge Act,
in order to improve the approach into the city, and the new
church was erected on the north-west side of the castle. The
ceremony of laying the foundation stone was performed by the
Right Rev. C. J. Blomfield, then Lord Bishop of the Diocese.
The length is about 90 feet, and the width 50, and the church
is calculated to contain 1000 persons. "It is rather a remarkable circumstance," says Hemingway, "that although Saint
Bridget's Parish, is wholly within the city, the ground occupied
by the church and cemetery is neither within the parish or the
city, but altogether within the county palatine; but by a clause
in the act, it is enacted, that after the consecration, it shall
'for all purposes, and to all intents whatsoever, be deemed
part of, and situated within the said parish of St. Bridget,
and within the said city of Chester.'"

The Rev. W. P. Hutton, M.A. is the present incumbent.

St. Michael's Church

Is situate on the east side of Bridge-street, opposite the end of Grosvenor-street leading to the New Bridge. The time of its foundation is uncertain, but it is supposed to have been connected with the monastery of St. Michael, which was given to the priory of Norton by Roger de Lacy in a charter, subsequently confirmed by Henry the Second; it is recorded by Bradshaw, that "the monastery of St. Michael was burnt by the great fire which happened on mid-lent sunday in 1118, at eight of the clock (all being in church), and consumed the greatest part of the city." It is conjectured that this monastery was situated in Bridge-street, in Rock's-court, where Dr. Williamson says "before it was converted into dwelling-houses, one might have beheld fair church-like windows, and other demonstrations of its being part of a religious house." The chancel was rebuilt in 1496, and enlarged in 1678. The old steeple, which was built in 1710, having fallen into decay from the perishable nature of the red sandstone, was taken down in 1849, and the present handsome structure, built with white stone, was erected in its place. The south, east, and a portion of the north walls of the church having also been found to be in a very defective state, they were taken down in 1850; in fact, the church has been almost entirely rebuilt, as none of the old walls remain, except the three internal arches, and a part of the north wall. The flat ceiling has been removed, but the nave and chancel roofs being principally constructed of oak and in a good state of preservation, have been retained; they have, however, been re-slated. The north chancel has been entirely rebuilt and new roofed. The north aisle of the nave is divided from the body of the church by three pointed arches springing from octagonal columns, the capitals being ornamented with quatrefoils. The interior of the old building was very inconvenient, unsightly, and dilapidated, but it is now completely restored in proper ecclesiastical style. The chancel is paved with beautiful tiles, those within the communion rails being liberally given by Mr. Minton. Each compartment of the five chancel windows is surrounded with a neat border of stained glass. The style of architecture adopted in the restoration of the church is the transition from the decorated to the perpendicular, that being considered as best suited to those portions of the old building which are retained. Great credit is due to Mr. James Harrison, the architect, for the very great skill and judgment he has displayed in the restoration of the church. The total cost is about £1700., of which the parishioners have borrowed £500. on the security of the church rates; about £900. has been raised by subscription, leaving a deficiency of about £300. Besides many smaller bequests from different individuals, this parish enjoys, under the will of Dr. Robert Oldfield, dated 24th April, 1695 "two-thirds of Dunham Hall and other lands and messuages at Dunham-on-the-Hill, together with lands at Boughton, for the purpose of paying £20. a year to the minister, provided he hold no other preferment, and of binding poor boys apprentices born in that parish, and of maintaining one or more poor boys, who should be apt to learn at the University." Owing to proper objects not having every year presented themselves, the revenues have accumulated, and with the bequeathed property now produce an annual rent of upwards of £400. The present trustees of Oldfield's Bequest are Henry Hesketh, T. Dixon, Esqrs. Major French, and Dr. R. P. Jones. St. Michael's is a perpetual curacy in the gift of the Bishop of Chester. The present incumbent is the Rev. James Haworth.

CHRIST CHURCH

Is situated in a thickly inhabited district called Newtown; the rapid increase in the population of this locality, rendering additional church accommodation necessary, the present edifice was erected to supply the need. It was consecrated on Oct. 23, 1838. The cost was £3390 (including £1000. for endowment, £100. for repair fund, &c.) The Rev. W. Gibson, formerly rector of St. Bride's, Chester, and now rector of Fawley, Hampshire, gave £1425; the Bishop of Chester (Dr. Sumner), the Rev. Chancellor Raikes, and Miss Rowe £100. each; H. Raikes, Esq. £55.; the late Gen. Beckwith £50.; W. Wardell, Esq. £50.; the Diocesan Church Building Society £500. The church is built in the early English style of architecture. Rev. R. E. Thomas is the present incumbent.

ST. PAUL'S CHURCH

Is situated near to Barrel well, Boughton, and was built by public subscription, under the patronage of Bishop Blomfield and Bishop Sumner. It was erected in 1830, at the cost of about £2000. It is capable of seating about 800 persons; 400 free sittings being appropriated for the poor. Under the church is a commodious room, which is occupied as a day and sabbath-school. There is no endowment on the church, the income of the minister being derived from the pew rents. The present incumbent is the Rev. J. Gaman, M.A.

ST. OLAVE'S CHURCH

Is situated on the east side of Lower Bridge-street, opposite

Castle-street. It is a small oblong structure, in outward appearance much resembling a barn. This church is of great antiquity, having been erected before the Norman Conquest. In the eleventh century it was possessed by the Botelars, by whom it was given, with two houses in the Market-place, to the Abbey of St. Werburgh, in 1101.

After the great civil war St. Olave's fell into disuse as a place of public worship, being only employed for baptisms and burials, on which occasions the minister of St. Michael's officiated. It was however re-opened as a parish church about the middle of last century, and continued so until the year 1841, when service in the church was discontinued, and the parish united with that of St. Michael's.

LITTLE ST. JOHN'S.

We refer the reader to the history we have already given of this ancient hospital and chapel in a former part of this work. The present incumbent is the Rev. William Clarke, B.D.

DISSENTING PLACES OF WORSHIP.

THE UNITARIAN CHAPEL

CLAIMS our first and most particular attention, not only as being the first dissenting place of worship in this city, and the parent trunk from which many others have branched forth, but also because of the important changes which mark its history. The following succinct sketch of the history of this place of worship is taken from Pigott's History of Chester. "The Unitarian Chapel is a large brick building, with a burial ground in front, situated between Crook Lane and Trinity Lane, having an entrance from each of those streets, and is generally called Crook's Lane Chapel. It was built in 1700, by a large, flourishing, respectable society, which had been formed in 1687 by the celebrated Matthew Henry, son of the learned, pious, and laborious Phillip Henry, one of the ejected ministers. In the register book belonging to the congregation of this place there is a short account of the rise, progress, and transactions of the society, written by Mr. Henry in 1710, being the twenty-third year of his ministry. From this account, it appears that

in 1682 there were three dissenting congregations in Chester
which had been founded by Mr. William Cook, Mr. Ralph
Hall, and Mr. John Harvey, ministers of the established church,
who had been ejected from their respective livings on account
of their non-compliance with the act of uniformity. After the
death of Mr. Cook and Mr. Hall, their congregations were
entirely broken up and dispersed by the persecutions of the
times, but such of them as continued dissenters occasionally
held meetings at each others houses, or joined Mr. Harvey's
congregation, which assembled at his house in a private manner,
in order to avoid the penalties which were then in force against
the nonconformists. James the Second, under the pretence of
universal toleration, but with a view to the establishment of
popery, granted them the liberty of public worship, of which
they had been deprived in the latter part of the reign of Charles
the Second. It was at this time that Mr. Henry, who began
his ministry in Chester, collected the remains of the congregation of Mr. Cook and Mr. Hall, and opened a meeting in White
Friars' lane. Mr. Harvey, who had been ejected from Wallasey,
in Cheshire, continued to preside over a dissenting congregation
in Bridge-street, for 13 years after toleration was granted; he
died November, 1699; he was succeeded by his son, who
resigned in 1706, on account of ill health. His congregation,
which was large and opulent, was united to that of Mr. Henry,
and in 1707, a large gallery was built on the south side of Crook's
Lane meeting house for their better accommodation. Thus the
three original nonconformist societies were united in one, under
the pastoral care of Mr. Henry, who was then the only dissenting minister in Chester."

Mr. Henry removed from Chester to Hackney in 1713, and
died of apoplexy, at Nantwich, where he had been on a visit
to his friends, in June, 1714, in the 52nd year of his age, and
was buried in Trinity church in this city. His exposition of
the Bible has gone through very many editions, and is still
in great repute with moderate Calvinists, both in the established
church and among the dissenters. Mr. John Gardiner succeeded
Mr. Henry in 1713, and held his appointment for more than
half a century. During the latter years of his ministry, his
religious opinions appear to have undergone a decided change,
departing very much from the doctrines maintained by Mr.
Henry, which gradually prepared the way for the full development of Unitarianism in the place by his successor Mr. Chidlaw,
who was an avowed believer and advocate of the tenets peculiar
to that system. The opinions of Unitarians being unpopular
here, the congregation is small. The present minister is the
Rev. James Malcolm.

INDEPENDENT CHAPEL.

This place of worship is situated on the west side of Queen Street. It is a handsome brick building, having a chaste stone front, with covered portico and pillars of the Grecian Doric order. It has galleries on three sides, and will accommodate about 1200 persons. The founders of this chapel were seceders from the Presbyterian congregation in Crook Street, in consequence of a departure from what they held as the principles of a sound faith, as we have already noticed. For some years they worshipped in a large room in Commonhall-street, afterwards occupied by Mr. Wilcoxon's congregation. They formed themselves into a church in 1772, when the Rev. Wm. Armitage was chosen the pastor. The chapel in Queen-street was erected in 1777; it was very much enlarged in 1838, when great improvements were made in the arrangements of the interior. At the same time, a spacious wing was added to the building, which is used as a lecture room, and as a Sabbath-school for girls: underneath the lecture room is a commodious Sabbath-school for boys. In addition to the schools meeting in Queen-street, there are also three branch schools in the suburbs of the city, which are supported by the congregation. The present minister is the Rev. Richard Knill.

WESLEYAN METHODIST CHAPEL.

(OLD CONNEXION.)

This chapel (says Hemingway) was erected in 1811; it is a large, well-built, handsome structure, with a semi-circular front, and two entrances. It is galleried on three sides, and behind the pulpit is a large orchestra for the accommodation of singers, where there is also a well-toned organ. The introduction of methodism into this city occurred about the year 1750, and the first preachèr who visited the neighbourhood was a Mr. John Bennett. He commenced his labours at Huntington Hall, in the neighbourhood, the residence of Mr. George Cotton; from thence the preaching was removed to the house of Mr. Richard Jones, in Love-lane, within this city, where a society was first formed; the house soon became too small for them, the society therefore procured and fitted up a capacious barn in Martin's Ash, from which time they were regularly supplied with travelling preachers, and where the Rev. John Wesley frequently visited them, in his annual excursions. After remaining in Martin's Ash for about 12 years, they had sufficient credit to obtain £520. upon bond, with which they erected, in 1765, the Octagon chapel, in Foregate-street, which they continued to occupy until their removal to St. John-street.

The Wesleyans have also built commodious school-rooms, which are very numerously attended.

WESLEYAN METHODIST CHAPEL.

(NEW CONNEXION.)

The new connexion methodists seceded from the old society on some points respecting the management of the funds, throwing open their financial matters to the knowledge and supervision of the people, and the general government of their societies. They have a large and elegant place of worship in Pepper-street, which is fronted with stone, and supported by four Corinthian pillars. The ministers are itinerant, and receive their appointment from the annual conference.

THE OCTAGON CHAPEL

Is situated in Foregate-street, and as already stated, was built in 1765, by the Wesleyan methodists. Upon their removal to St. John-street, it was purchased and has since that time been occupied by its present possessors. The congregation was collected by the labours of the late Rev. P. Oliver, a clergyman of the established church, who embraced the doctrines of the celebrated Mr. Whitfield. This gentleman (says Hemingway, from whom we quote) converted some outbuildings near his house in Boughton into a chapel, where he officiated until his death, without any other reward than the gratification of diffusing among his poor neighbours, according to the best of his judgment, the spirit and principles of evangelical truth. At his death, he bequeathed the chapel to his congregation, for a term of years; but upon their removal to the Octagon, they sold the interest on it, and it has since been occasionally used as a place of worship by the Independents of Queen-street. The congregation at the Octagon is in connexion with the societies which were under the patronage of the late Countess of Huntington. The present minister is the Rev. W. Evans.

THE BAPTIST'S CHAPEL

Is situated in Hamilton place; it is a small brick building, erected in 1806. The Rev. W. Giles is the present officiating minister, and the congregation is small.

WELSH CALVINISTIC CHAPEL

Stands on the north side of Commonhall-street; it was opened for public service on the 12th November, 1820. The public service is conducted in the Welsh language.

COMMONHALL-STREET CHAPEL

Was erected in 1841, by the congregation of the late Mr.

Jonathan Wilcoxon, who officiated in an adjoining room, without pecuniary emolument, for 37 years. After his death the congregation united themselves with the Independents.

QUAKERS' MEETING HOUSE

Is a plain building standing on the east side of Frodsham-street. It is capable of containing several hundred persons, and has a burial ground in front; it is one of the oldest dissenting places of worship now existing in Chester. Clarkson in his memoirs of William Penn, says "among the places he (Willm. Penn) visited in Cheshire, was Chester itself. The king (James the Second) who was then travelling, arriving there at the same time, went to the *Meeting House* of the Quakers to hear him preach." In George Fox's journal, there is an entry which proves that the Quakers have existed as a distinct society in Chester for about 200 years. Under date 1657, he writes "from Wrexham we came to west Chester, and it being the fair time, we staid there awhile and *visited Friends*." The resident members of this society are now very few, and the service is seldom performed.

THE PRIMITIVE METHOTISTS

Have a small chapel in Steam-Mill-street, erected about the year 1825, and the members of the society appear to be on the increase.

ROMAN CATHOLIC CHAPEL

Is situated on the west side of Queen-street. It is a small but handsome brick building, with an elegant Doric portico, supported by four light stone pillars in front, and was built in 1799. The chapel is now found to be too small for the congregation, and the erection of a larger edifice is contemplated when the requisite funds can be provided. Rev. J. Carberry is the present priest.

PRESBYTERIAN CHAPEL

Is situated in Pepper-street. It was erected in 1827 by the Baptists, but the congregation becoming very small, it was closed some years ago. In 1846, it was re-opened for Presbyterian worship, and has continued to be occupied by a small but respectable society. The chapel is built of stone in a neat style. Rev. D. Blelock is the minister.

ENDOWED AND CHARITABLE SCHOOLS.

THE KING'S SCHOOL.

HIS school was founded by King Henry VIII, in the 36th year of his reign, for twenty-four boys to receive £3 4s. 0d. each, who are appointed by the Dean and Chapter. By the charter it is ordained, "that there ever be in our church of Chester twenty-four boys, poor and friendless, to be maintained out of the income of our church, of good .capacities and given to learning if possible; which, however, we would not have admitted before they can read and write, and somewhat understand the rudiments of grammar; and this at the discretion of the Dean and Head Master. And these boys we will have maintained at the expense of our church until they have made some tolerable proficiency in the Latin grammar, and have been taught to write and speak Latin, for which end they are allowed the term of four years, or if the Dean or Head Master see cause, of five and no more. But we order that no one, unless he be a chorister of our church, be elected a poor scholar that is under the age of nine years." Some important alterations have recently been made in the management of the school, which have very considerably increased its efficiency. We are happy to find that the inhabitants of Chester are availing themselves of the great advantages provided by this excellent institution. The course of instruction has been made such as to qualify the scholars for any of the literary professions or commercial pursuits, embracing as it does, all the elements of a sound mathematical, classical, and general education. The Head Master is the Rev. R. W. Gleadowe, M.A., and the second master the Rev. F. Grosvenor, B.A. The chorister boys are educated apart, by a master expressly appointed for that purpose by the Dean and Chapter.

DIOCESAN SCHOOL.

This institution was established January 2, 1812, by public subscription, under the patronage of the Bishop of Chester. It is situated on the south side of the top of George-street, is 80 feet long by 33 wide, and is capable of accommodating 400 children. It is supported by benefactions and annual subscriptions, and the institution is in a most prosperous condition; its object is to promote a good education among the children of the poor. According to the last report the number of boys taught in this school is 178; total number of boys who are and have been

instructed, 2944. The present master is Mr. Beswick, who is efficiently fulfilling the duties of his office.

THE MARQUIS AND MARCHIONESS OF WESTMINSTER'S SCHOOLS.

This is a fine lofty building, situated on the north side of St. John's churchyard, and was erected in the year 1813 for the gratuitous education of the children of the poor. It consists of two stories, the lower one of which is occupied by boys, and the upper one by girls. Both rooms are fitted up in a complete style, and are capable of containing 800 children. Mr. Pearson is the present master.

There are also the Blue Coat school, established by Bishop Stratford, in 1700. The Blue Girl's school, established in 1721. Infant schools established in 1825, under the patronage of Bishop Blomfield. Diocesan Training college, erected in 1742, of which the Principal is the Rev. Arthur Rigg, M.A., the Vice-Principal the Rev. W. J. Constable, B. A. For a full description of this important institution, we refer the reader to a former part of this work.

CHARITABLE INSTITUTIONS.

The General Infirmary.—Chester Humane Society.—The Female Penitentiary.—Female House of Refuge.

———

Before the visitor leaves this ancient and interesting city, we have no doubt he will be induced to visit

EATON HALL,

The princely mansion of the Marquis of Westminster, which is situated in a beautiful park, about three miles to the south of Chester. The principal approach to the House is through the Chester gateway—an exquisite building, situated within a short distance of the town. The design is a spirited copy of St. Agustine's Abbey Gate, Canterbury, by T. Jones, Esq. architect, of Chester, who has added appropriate wings and wing walls, after the style of architecture in the thirteenth century. The approach is from a noble esplanade, about 200 feet long by 100 feet broad, at the further end of which the lodge is entered through a pointed arch and groining, enriched with groups of very delicate foliage. Each side of the archway is defended by an octagonal tower, 50 feet high, rising about 12 feet above the centre of the edifice. The lower parts of the towers with the wings are comparatively plain; the centre of them is enriched with niches surmounted by bunches of foliage exquisitely carved; the upper part is richly pannelled and pierced, which combined with the battlements produce a light effect. The middle, above the archway and between the

tower, is enriched with two windows, surrounded by elegant
mouldings with a central niche containing the Westminster
arms, supported by the talbots in grand relief.   Above the
windows are a series of grotesque heads and fretwork, surrounded with an enriched battlement.   The sides of the upper
part are carried through in the same style, but not so highly
enriched.   The lodge or wing portions have a window in front,
surmounted with a cornice and an appropriate battlement having angular buttresses.   The inner front on the Eaton side is
ornamented in the same manner.   To the sides are attached
wing walls extending 60 feet, pierced with loop-holes and
embattled, forming a grand *tout ensemble.*

The present magnificent edifice, the designs for which
were furnished by Pordon, was erected upon the site of the old
hall (a stately brick mansion, built by Sir John Vanburgh, taken
down in 1803), and is considered the most splendid modern
specimen of the pointed Gothic in the kingdom.   Although in
the general design the florid Gothic order of the time of Edward
III. has been followed, the architect has, in parts, not only
availed himself of the low Tudor arch, but has adopted the
peculiar style of any period suitable to his purpose, and has
made subservient to modern domestic convenience, the rich and
varied forms in which our ancient ecclesiastical architecture
abounds.   The walls, battlements, and pinnacles of the building
are constructed of stone of a light and beautiful colour—brought
from Delamere Forest—and round the turrets and in various
parts of the parapets are shields charged in relief, with the
heraldic achievements of the house of Grosvenor, and of other
ancient families with whom they are allied.   The building
consists of a centre and two wings, the latter differing from
each other somewhat in design ; of these, that to the south,
composed of two compartments, is the more beautiful ; this
wing is oblong and angular, with four octagonal turrets at the
corners, buttresses at the sides, and having the embattled
parapets surmounted with pinnacles ; the decorations are rich
to profusion, but every part accords with the original plan.
The eastern and western fronts agree in their general form
and proportions, but the former possesses the greater number
of minute decorations.   In the front a cloister extends along
the entire length between the two spacious windows of the
dining and drawing rooms, and conducts to the terrace : from
the terrace, which is 350 feet long, the view is eminently
beautiful.   The groves and gardens, with the conservatory,
form the foreground ; beyond them is seen the noble inlet of
the Dee, and a charming extensive landscape fills up the distance.   The view from the gardens embraces the south or

library wing, but the opposite extremity is partly hidden by the trees; beyond it, but apparently mingling with the turrets and pinnacles, is seen a lofty octagonal clock-tower, connected by flying buttresses, with four slender shafts on a square basement; it is attached to part of the stable court, which recedes from the line of the east front, and which is of great extent.

The principal entrance is on the western front, under a lofty portico, the clustered pillars of which support a beautifully groined ceiling; from this a flight of steps leads to a pair of massive bronzed doors admitting to the grand entrance hall, which is elegant and lofty, occupying the height of two stories; it is 41 feet long and 31 feet in breadth, and has a groined ceiling, embellished with the armorial bearings of the house of Grosvenor, and other devices in the bosses that cover the juncture of the ribs. The branching compartments terminate in a rich centre piece, from which is suspended a beautiful lamp, which, when lighted gives the pavement, composed of the choicest marbles, a gorgeous effect; the floor was laid down at a cost of 1600 guineas. The screen at the end of the hall is decorated with shields of arms, and consists of five arches, which support a gallery connecting the sleeping apartments on the north and south sides of the house, which are separated by the elevation of the hall. In lofty canopied recesses at the sides of the hall, are four complete suits of ancient armour, and beneath the gallery two open arches to the right and left conduct to the grand staircase and the state bed-room. Through a pair of massive richly carved mahogany folding-doors, which cost 100 guineas each, the visitor is ushered into the saloon, which forms the centre of a suite of apartments of unequalled beauty and magnificence. The groined and fretted ceilings of these rooms, decorated with the endless ramifications of fanwork tracery and the most beautiful varieties of Gothic foliage, brilliant in colour and rich with the herald's skill, yet chastened by the direction of an exquisite taste, and subdued by the propriety of the arrangement—the walls beautified in the richest style of decoration, receiving and reflecting still more glowing hues as the sunbeams stream through the painted glass, with which the windows are profusely ornamented—the paintings of the first-rate excellence—the chandeliers of elaborate workmanship—the gorgeous furniture corresponding with the house—the cabinets of Mosaic ivory and pearl—the golden vases sparkling in the niche—in short, the whole finishing and furnishing of these apartments constitute a combination of costliness and good taste which justly commands the admiration of every visitor.

The *saloon* is a splendid apartment; it is a square of 30 feet, formed into an octagon by arches across the angles, which give to the vaultings a beautiful form; there are three windows, enriched with tracery, and nearly filled with painted glass, through which a subdued light is admitted, giving to the Gothic character of the saloon a very rich and striking effect. The elegant fan tracery of the ceiling is supported by twelve slender columns in the angles and sides; the Roman circle forming the centre, is composed of numerous mouldings and ornamented with fruit and foliage. The stained glass windows represent the heraldic achievements of the noble house of Grosvenor, with those of the ancient families with whom they have formed alliances, and in the upper compartments are six full length figures of William the Conqueror, Sir Gilbert le Grosvenor, his companion at the time of the Norman invasion, and the nephew of Hugh Lupus, the lady of Sir Gilbert, Sir Robert le Grosvenor the crusader, Joan Lady Grosvenor, heiress of Eaton, and Odo, Bishop of Bayeux, uncle of the conqueror. The furniture of the room is chaste, both in colour and design. The chimney-piece is of statuary marble, and opposite to it is an organ, both highly adorned. This room has recently been richly decorated in the Alhambresque style, by Mr. John Morris of this city; each panel being most beautifully painted with Moorish scenery.

The ante-rooms, though of similar proportions, are differently decorated; the ceiling of each is covered with a delicate pattern of tracery, and both are superbly furnished. The windows are composed of stained glass, representing the figures and arms of six of the Earls of Chester.

The ante-dining-room is a handsome apartment, recently decorated in the Alhambresque style, by Mr. Morris, though with less elaborate finish than the saloon.

The dining-room is well proportioned, being 50 feet by 37 feet. The simplicity of its design is not owing to any deficiency of ornament, on the contrary, its several enrichments are gorgeous; but in comparison with the other state apartments, which are profusely decorated, it is characterized by a simplicity peculiarly elegant. Springing from the corners of the room, four ribs extend their ramified tracery over the ceiling, in the centre of which their borders of wreathed foliage unite, and thence from a richly carved boss is suspended a large and noble chandelier. The sideboard stands in an arched and highly enriched recess, and placed at each end of the room are two canopied niches, containing a colossal statue by *Westmacott.* At the lower end are those of Sir Robert le Grosvenor, who distinguished himself in the crusades, and of

Mary, Lady Grosvenor at the time of the revolution. Those at the upper end of the room represent Sir Gilbert le Grosvenor, who came over from France at the time of the Norman invasion, with his uncle Hugh Lupus, and Joan or Jane Lady Grosvenor, heiress of Eaton in the reign of Edward IV. The room contains full-length portraits of the late Marquis and Marchioness of Westminster, by *Jackson, R.A.* Abigail meeting David, by *Rubens*, and the Judgment of Paris, after Rubens, by *Peters*. The walls of the dining-room are richly ornamented.

The ante-drawing-room is very elegant; its decorations in the Alhambresque style are peculiarly rich. It contains three most beautiful book-cases, chaste in design and exquisitely finished.

The drawing-room has four magnificent niches, and a noble window with a lofty pointed arch and tracery of rich and beautiful forms, adorned with stained glass. It is placed at the end opposite the entrance, and commands a fine prospect, the inlet of the Dee forming a conspicuous object in the landscape. The pattern of the ceiling, which is decorated with compartments numerously subdivided and intersected, is formed in four divisions issuing from clustered pillars with foliated capitals, and united in the centre to an hexagonal frame elaborately reticulated, from which issues a pendant of foliage sustaining a superb chandelier of crystal. The number and variety of the carved knots and foliage add to the beauty of the ceiling, but the decorations that increase its effect, and are indeed its most prominent attractions, are the shields on which the heraldic achievements of the various branches of the Grosvenor family are emblazoned. The pale hue of the ceiling, the gorgeous decorations in the centre, and the rich glow of the crimson velvet with which the walls of this noble apartment are covered, all combine to render it a scene of unsurpassed magnificence. Corresponding in costly embellishment with its architecture is the furniture of blue satin, fringed with yellow silk, crimson velvet, and damask satin. Over the chimney-piece, which is carved in statuary marble, is a lofty mirror in an arched frame, sufficiently broad to admit a pattern of tracery, on the compartments of which crimson velvet is introduced with happy effect. This splendid apartment contains the following pictures:—Judith with the head of Holofernes, *Guercino*—Reuben shewing to Jacob the bloody garment of his son Joseph, also by *Guercino.*—Antiochus and Stratonice, *Pietro de Cortona.*—Christ and the Woman of Samaria, *Mignard.*—Jacob blessing Ephraim and Manasseh, *West.*—Elijah raising the Widow's Son, also by *West.*

The library comprehends the whole of the south wing, and is the most spacious room in the mansion; it varies in breadth, but is 120 feet long. The bookcases are of rich carved oak, and the windows are ornamented with tracery and stained glsss. When the door is thrown open, the view from the further end of the library is continued through the vaulted corridor at the opposite extremity of the house, a length of 480 feet. A very rare piece of antiquity is preserved in the library, it is a gold torque, an ornament of dignity worn by the ancient Britons; it is wreathed, the rods are linked together in a circle, and it measures 10 or 11 inches in diameter. The library contains many most valuable and rare books and MSS., among which may be mentioned—a copy of the chronicle of Henry of Huntingdon, in which is a curious drawing of the entry of King Stephen into Lincoln; an illuminated MS. on vellum, containing the proceedings of the celebrated suit of arms between Scroope and Grosvenor; and (among other Cheshire MSS.) one volume of collections, containing a transcript of a large portion of the celebrated and lost record, distinguished by the name of "the Cheshire Doomsday;" also the confirmation charter of Chester Cathedral by the second Ranulf, surnamed De Gernon or Gernons, Earl of Chester, in which the grant of Hugh Lupus is recapitulated.

The great staircase is very richly decorated : at the top of the first flight of stairs are three niches with statues. On the opposite side, at the foot of the stairs, is an arcade supporting the upper floor, and from these arches, which have open spandrils, the best view of this magnificent staircase is obtained.

The state bed-room is an elegant apartment; the ceiling is vaulted, and the bed is of mahogany and groined; its principal carved ornaments appear on clustered pillars, detached from the corners. The sofas are of blue satin, in richly carved and gilt frames, and the other seats are covered in finely wrought needlework of various colours. Over the chimney-piece is a mirror, the frame of which is composed of handsomely clustered pillars, pinnacles, and crocketed canopies, the whole being richly decorated with gilding, and minutely carved.

The tenants' hall is under the library, and corresponds with it in extent; it is used for the entertainment of the tenantry. The windows are enriched with tracery, and four massy clustered pillars sustain the arches and groins of the ceiling, which is remarkably flat, when the breadth of its span is taken into consideration.

The chapel is a small, beautifully proportioned edifice ; there is no gallery, the noble family and the domestics all being seated on the groud floor. The windows are beautifully ornamented with stained glass, the work of Mr. Bollantine.

The east front of the hall is adorned with a raised terrace, from whence sloping to an extensive piece of water; and intersected by walks, extend the flower gardens and pleasure grounds, which cover a space of fifty acres.   The extensive pleasure grounds and gardens are laid out in admirable taste; the conservatory, recently erected, is a most beautiful construction, and forms an attractive object.   At the termination of a fine gravel walk, and opposite to the conservatory, a Gothic temple has been built for the reception of a Roman altar, discovered near Chester, 1821.   The Mosaic pavement of the temple was brought from a palace of the Emperor Tiberius, in the island of Caprie, by Lord Robert Grosvenor.

The stables, which form a large quadrangle on the north side of the hall, are erected in a style of architecture correspondent with that of the house, and are separated from it by a small shrubbery.

An elegant iron bridge of 150 feet span, crossing the river Dee which runs through a part of the grounds, is likewise a real embellishment to the landscape.   This bridge is exceedingly ornamental; it was erected by Hazledine, at an expense of about £8000.   From each point of which Eaton Hall is approached, it presents a picture of unusual architectural grandeur; the scenery by which the hall is surrounded heightens the effect; westward, the view embraces the mountains of Wales, and to the east appear the Peckforton hills, with the bold rock on which stands the ruins of Beeston Castle.   The river Dee, winding in various directions, imparts great beauty to the varied and extensive landscape.

The noble house of Grosvenor traces its descent through a long line of illustrious ancestors, who flourished in Normandy with dignity and splendour, from the time it was created a sovereign Dukedom, in the year 912, to the conquest of England in 1066, always ranking with the first nobles, and having had the government of many castles and strongholds in that duchy. The founder of this ancient house was uncle of Rollo, the famous Dane, and was one of the principal commanders who, in the year 876, accompanied him in his invasion of England. William seventh Duke of Normandy, at the time of his descent upon England in 1066, was accompanied by his twin brother Robert, afterwards Earl of Cornwall, and Odo, Bishop of Bayeux, afterwards Earl of Kent ; he had also, for his immediate attendants, his nephew Hugh Lupus, afterwards Earl of Chester, and Gilbert le Grosvenor, nephew to Hugh.

The present most noble Marquis succeeded to the title in 1845, and is the twenty-second in descent from Gilbert le Grosvenor, the companion in arms of William the Conqueror.   His lordship, who holds the distinguished office of Lord Lieutenant

of Cheshire, married in 1819, Elizabeth Mary, youngest daughter
of the Duke of Sutherland, and has, with other issue, a son
and heir, Hugh Lupus, Earl Grosvenor, one of the representatives in parliament for Chester, for which so many members
of this illustrious house have been chosen.*

ECCLESTON

Is a beautiful little village, about two miles from Chester,
much resorted to by the inhabitants of that city, and by
strangers, from its vicinity to Eaton Hall. The chief object
of attraction is the church, built in 1810 by the Marquis of
Westminster; it is an elegant Gothic structure, and has been
considered by men of taste as one of the best specimens in
the kingdom. The interior of the church is chaste and elegant:
in the north transept is the mausoleum of the Eaton family,
and opposite to it their pew: over the altar is a fine painting
by Westall, of Joseph of Arimathea begging the body of Christ.
The houses in the village are neat, and chiefly built in the
Gothic style, to harmonize with the church, and also with the
mansion of its munificent owner. There is a very good inn
here, the Grosvenor Arms, where visitors may have refreshment at very moderate charges.

* The year before the extensive alterations were commenced in this
magnificent mansion, the noble Marquis arranged that visitors should be
admitted only by tickets, which were obtained of the publisher of this
work and at the hotels, and that the money realized by their sale should
be appropriated to the charitable institutions in Chester; by this truly
praiseworthy scheme, the goodly sum of £200. was made available for
benevolent purposes, which rendered timely aid to the following excellent
objects:—Chester Infirmary £50; Improvement of the Cathedral £50;
House Refuge £25; Penitentiary £25; Blue Coat Hospital £25; and
the Infant School £25. When the improvements, now in progress, are
completed, whe have no doubt that the same admirable arrangement
will be continued.

REPRESENTATIVES IN PARLIAMENT,

FOR THE CITY OF CHESTER, FROM THE REVOLUTION IN 1688.

1 Wm. and Mary.—Sir Thos. Grosvenor, Bart.; Richard Leving, Esq.

7 Wm. III.—Sir Thos. Grosvenor, Bart.; Roger Whitley, Esq.; on whose death was substituted Thomas Cowper, Esq.

10 Wm. III.—Sir Thos. Grosvenor, Bart.; Peter Shakerley, Esq.

12 Wm. III.—Sir Henry Bunbury, Bart.; Peter Shakerley, Esq.

13 William III.—The same.

1 Anne.—The same.

4 Anne.—Sir Henry Bunbury, Bart; Peter Shakerley, Esq.

7 Anne.—The same.

9 Anne.—The same.

12 Anne.—The same.

1 Geo. I.—Sir Henry Bunbury; Sir Richd. Grosvenor.

8 Geo. I.—The same.

1 Geo. II.—Sir Richard Grosvenor, Baronet ; Thomas Grosvenor, Esq. ; on whose deaths, July, 1732, and January, 1732-3, were substituted Robert Grosvenor, Esq. and Sir Charles Bunbury, Bart.

8 Geo. II.—Sir Robert Grosvenor, Bart.; Sir Charles Bunbury, Bart.

15 Geo. II.—The same. On the death of Sir Chas. Bunbury, April, 1742, was substituted Philip H. Warburton, Esq.

21 Geo. II.—Sir Robert Grosvenor, Bart.; Philip Henry Warburton, Esq.

27 Geo. II.—Sir Robert Grosvenor, Bart. ; Richard Grosvenor, Esq. On the death of Sir Robert Grosvenor, August, 1755, was substituted Thomas Grosvenor, Esq.

1 Geo. III.—Thomas Grosvenor, Esq.; R. Wilbraham Bootle, Esq.

8 Geo. III.—The same.

15 Geo. III.—The same.

21 Geo. III.—The same.

24 Geo. III.—The same.

30 Geo. III.—Thomas Grosvenor, Esq.; Robert Viscount Belgrave. On the death of Thos. Grosvenor, Esq., 1795, was substituted Thomas Grosvenor, Esq.

36 Geo. III.—Thomas Grosvenor, Esq. ; Lord Viscount Belgrave.

42 Geo. III.—The same. On Lord Belgrave's succession to the Earldom of Grosvenor, 1802, was substituted Richard Earl Drax Grosvenor, Esq.

47 Geo. III.—Thomas Grosvenor, Esq.; Richard Earl Drax Grosvenor, Esq.

47 Geo. III.—Thos. Grosvenor, Esq. ; John Egerton, Esq.

53 Geo. III.—The same.

59 Geo. III.—Thomas Grosvenor, Esq. ; Lord Viscount Belgrave.

1 Geo. IV.—The same.

7 Geo. IV.—Lord Viscount Belgrave ; Right Hon. Robert Grosvenor.

1 Will. IV.—Right Hon. Robert Grosvenor ; Sir Philip Grey Egerton, Bart.

1 Will. IV.—Right Hon. Robert Grosvenor ; F. Cunliffe Offley, Esq.

2 Will. IV.—Right Hon. Robert Grosvenor ; John Finchett-Maddock, Esq.

4 Will. IV.—Right Hon. Robert Grosvenor ; John Jervis, Esq.

5 Will. IV.—The same.

1 Vic. I.—The same.

4 Vic. I.—The same. Lord Grosvenor retired in 1846, and Earl Grosvenor was substituted.

11 Vic. I.—Sir John Jervis (the Attorney-General) ; Earl Grosvenor; Sir John Jervis retired in 1850, and the Hon. W. O. Stanley was substituted.

CHRONOLOGY.

the standard-bearer, the Welsh, under the sons of Owen Gwynedd, were victorious.—Henry II. received at Chester the homage of Malcolm, king of Scotland.

1180 The greater part of Chester destroyed by fire.

1181 Earl Hugh the second died at Leeke.

1198 Henry de Lacy, constable of Chester, collecting a vast body of players, fiddlers, and other loose persons, at Chester midsummer fair, compels Llewelyn to raise the siege of Rhuddlan Castle, in which Earl Randal the Third was besieged, and in great straits.

1211 King John visits Chester.

1224 An assessment for repairing the walls.

1232 Earl Randal the Third died at Wallingford, in Berkshire. Buried in the chapter-house, Chester.

1237 John Scott, last Earl of Chester, died at Dernhall, June 7th.—Hugh le Despences, Stephen de Segrave, and Henry de Audley, put in charge of the castle.

1256 Prince Edward here on the festival of St. Kenelm; he stayed three days, and received the homage of the Welsh and Cheshire nobility.

1257 The Welsh, under Llewelyn, ravage the country to the very gates of the city.—The king summoned his barons to meet him here.—Government of the city invested in a mayor and sheriffs.

1264 The city greatly strengthened by William de Zouch, justice of Chester.—The Earl of Derby, with a great army, takes possession of the city and castle for the barons.

1265 Duke de Taney, the barons' justice, besieged for eight weeks, without effect, in the castle.

1275 The king directs the citizens to provide two ships for the Scotch wars.

1276 King Edward the First here on his way against Llewelyn.

1277 King Edward again here on his way to Rhuddlan castle, which he took; and ordered that all in Cheshire that could spend £20. per annum should be made knights.

1278 Dee bridge overthrown by a great flood.—The city reduced almost to ruins by a dreadful fire.

1279 Dee bridge rebuilt.

1282 King Edward here from June 6th to July 4th.

1283 The King and his Queen Eleanor heard mass in the Cathedral, after his successes against the Welsh and the birth of Edward Prince of Wales. He gave the monks an altar-cloth of great value.

1284 The King here for four days in September.

1294 The King passed through Chester, to quell Madoc's rebellion.

1300 The Welsh nobility did final homage to Edward of Caer-
narvon in the castle.

1310 Henry Lacy, Earl of Lincoln and Constable of Chester,
died in London.

1312 Edward the Second met Gaveston in Chester, on his return
from banishment in Ireland.

1321 A murage duty of a farthing in 20s. granted here and at
Frodsham, for repairing the walls and paving the city.

1322 Water Tower built for £100.

1349 The Mayor slain by Richard Ditton, who was pardoned
on paying 150 marks.

1353 The Black Prince and an armed force came here to protect
the justices against a commotion, caused by the dearness
of provisions.

1356 A Mayor's feast, comprising all the dainties of the season,
cost only 11s. 10d.

1379 A bushel of wheat sold for 6d.; a gallon of white wine
for 6d.; a gallon of claret for 4d.; a fat goose for 2d.;
and a fat pig for 1d.

1393 Sir Baldwyn Rudistone and other desperadoes, excite a
dreadful riot in the city. They were finally expelled, but
returned a few days after with three hundred men, and
attempted to take the place by surprise, but were repulsed,
and many taken prisoners.

1394 Richard the Second came to Chester on his way to Ireland.

1398 Chester erected into a principality.—Richard the Second
present at the installation of John Baughall, Bishop of
Lichfield and Coventry, at St. John's.

1399 Henry of Lancaster mustered his troops under the walls,
and marched against Richard the Second, whom he took
at Flint; returned to Chester and lodged the unfortunate
monarch in the castle.—The Duke of Surrey imprisoned
in the castle for bringing a messuage from the King.

1405 A pardon granted to the citizens for joining in Henry
Percy's rebellion; but the Mayor was superseded.

1409 John Ewloe, Mayor, was removed from the government
of the city, which was transferred to Sir. W. Brereton,
a military officer.

1431 Great frost for nine weeks.

1435 A great dearth: the people made bread of peas, *feathers,*
and fern roots.

1441 Rockley and Rooley, gaolers of the castle and Northgate,
fought a pitched battle on the Roodee.

1447 Eleanor, Duchess of Gloucester, confined in the castle for
practising the King's death.

1455 Queen Margaret, consort of Henry the Sixth, at Chester.

1463 Several citizens of Chester slain at Mold, by Rinalt of the Tower, and the Mayor hung on a staple in his hall.

1470 Henry the Sixth at Chester, confers the shrievalty of Cheshire on William Stanley, of Hooton.

1474 Edward, Prince of Wales, son of Edward the Fourth, came to Chester about Christmas, and conveyed to the castle in great pomp.

1489 A goose was eaten on the top of St. Peter's steeple, by the parson and his friends.—Hugh Dutton, the sword-bearer, had his meat, drink, &c. given from the Mayor, and 13s. 4d. out of the treasury allowed him.

1491 Simon Ripley, abbot of St. Werburgh's died.—A great tempest on St. John's day.

1493 A great fire without the Northgate.—John Puleston, Esq. of Wrexham, almost killed one Patrick, at the high altar of the abbey, and so suspended the services of the church.

1494 King Henry the Seventh and the king's mother came here, and many lords with them, on their way to visit the Earl of Derby, at Hawarden castle.

1496 The steeple of the White Friars built, and the chancel of St. Michael's church.

1498 Prince Arthur visited Chester from August 4 to September 9. The midsummer show was performed before the Prince at the Abbey-gate. August 25, he created the Mayor an Esquire.

1500 The further end of Dee bridge rebuilt.—A great fire without the Northgate.

1503 All innkeepers ordered to hang out lanterns from All Saints to Candlemas. Taverns to close at nine o'Clock.

1504 Pavement laid from the High Cross to the Eastgate and to St. Michael's.

1505 The city made a distinct county.

1506 Old steeple of St. Werburgh taken down.

1507 The sweating sickness prevalent; only four women died.

1509 First stone of the new steeple of St. Werburgh laid.

1515 An affray between the citizens and some Welshmen at St. Werburgh's-lane.

1517 Great plague visitation; grass grew a foot high at the cross, and other streets in the city.

1522 Sixty men sent from the city to assist the Earl of Surrey's army against the Scots.—Henry the Eighth ordered all citizens to remain within the city for the defence thereof.

1523 A charter granted to the citizens, exempting them from being impressed.

1529 The play of Robert Cecil acted at the High Cross, then newly gilt.

1532 Mr. Massey, of Puddington, being searcher, brought in
certain Spaniards to the castle, for having killed one of
his company. The Mayor stopped him, which had like
to have caused great slaughter, had not great help been.
It has been erroneously said that this was the cause of
the city Sheriffs having to execute county criminals.

1533 Decreed that the common council shall for the future be
elected by the corporation in assembly, and not nominated as heretofore by the Mayor.

1536 Sir W. Brereton, chamberlain of Chester, put to death
the 17th of May, for matters concerning Queen Anne.

1537 Water first brought from Boughton to the Bridge-gate by
pipes.—The nunneries and other religious houses suppressed.

1539 Conduit made at the Dee bridge by Dr. Wall.

1540 Bishopric of Chester instituted, July 10.

1541 Ordered, that when any of the common council die, others
shall be chosen in their places, of the "saddest and
most substantial citizens."

1545 The common hall was built and made out of St. Nicholas's
chapel.

1549 A skirmish between the citizens and 500 Irish kerns;
the latter much beaten.

1550 The sweating sickness and great scarcity.

1551 Dreadful flood at Saltney; many people drowned in their
beds, and timber trees left on the top of Dee bridge.

1553 Queen Mary ordered the Mayor to expel Thos. Glaziour
from his place as clerk of the pentice, which was refused to be done.

1554 George Marsh burnt at Boughton for the profession of
the gospel.

1556 Country bakers invited to attend the market. A bushel
of wheat sold at sixteen shillings.

1560 Peter Colman, a freeman, disfranchised for allowing a
non-freeman to trade in his name.

1563 "The History of Eneas and Queen Dido" played on the
Roodee, the Sunday after midsummer day, on which
occasion there were two forts made, and shipping in the
water, beside horsemen well appointed.

1564 Great fire without the Northgate; 33 houses, besides
barns and other buildings, destroyed.

1566 Great fire in Handbridge.

1568 Northgate-street, White Friars-lane, Parsons-lane, and
Castle-lane paved.

1569 The Sheriffs fought, and broke their wands on each
other; they were committed to the Northgate, and fined
£10. towards mending the walls.

1571 The Whitsun plays acted; an inhibition from the bishop arrived too late.

1573 The mayor removed the corn market to the Abbey side. The Dean and Chapter committed the workmen to the castle for three days.

1574 A conduit made at the Cross, neatly ornamented with carved work.—Two sides of St. John's steeple fell down and destroyed great part of the west end of the church. A plague began in Chester; only a few persons died.

1575 The sheriffs committed to the Northgate for refusing to levy estreats.—A collection made for building a house of correction under the Northgate.—The corn market ordered to be held in the Northgate ditch, under the walls.

1576 The privy council ordered the Mayor to discharge a man confined in the Northgate, for asserting that Queen Elizabeth had two bastards by the Earl of Leicester.

1577 The whole company of butchers committed to the Northgate, for not providing a sufficient quantity of meat for the use of the city.

1579 Watergate-street paved at the cost of the residents, for the space before their own houses.

1580 Eighteen yards of St. Peter's spire rebuilt.

1581 St. John's church granted to the parishioners, who rebuilt the dilapidated choir.

1583 The crosses at the Bars, the Northgate, and the Spital chapel pulled down.

1584 Dreadful hailstorm; much harm done to the mills by the floods, and many cattle killed by lightning.

1585 Sixteen pirates stole a ship from Wirral, and killed a man; the wind forcing the vessel back, they were apprehended and committed to the Northgate.—Castle bridge fell in; two horses and other cattle killed.

1586 A rumour in the night that seven hundred Spaniards had landed at the New Quay, which rose all the city in a fright, but it was not so.

1587 A coiner hung, drawn, and quartered, and his quarters set on the four gates.

1589 A woman burnt at Boughton for poisoning her husband. —The keeper of the castle gaol hung for killing a prisoner.

1590 An order made that none should be made free except he came in armour or other furniture, and depose that it was not borrowed.

1591 The gate at the Abbey-square began to be built.

1593 The aldermen compelled to reside in the city.

1594 An army of 4000 horse and foot passed through Chester on their way to Ireland, to quell the rebellion of Tyrone.

I

1595 Ale to be sold three pints for a penny.—1700 horse and foot passed through on their way to Ireland.

1598 Seven hundred horse and foot, and 200 carriage horses shipped for Ireland.—The Earl of Essex splendidly treated by the Mayor.

1599 The plays and old customs of the city altered by the Mayor; the bull ring taken up, and the procession of the shows prohibited.—5930 horse and foot shipped at different periods this year for Ireland.

1600 An admiralty warrant disobeyed as an encroachment on the city's privileges.—2290 soldiers shipped for Ireland.

1601 The causeway broken down, and the mills stopped for three months.—4051 soldiers shipped for Ireland.

1602 A passage made for carts through the Newgate, at the expense of the inhabitants of St. John's-lane.—The plague broke out in St. John's-lane; 60 a week died; no fairs held.—Lord Mountjoy, with the Earl of Tyrone prisoner, arrived here on his way to London, and slept at the Mayor's house.

1603 Eight hundred and twelve persons died of the plague.— Many citizens lived in tents under the New Tower.

1604 The Cathedral bells new cast.—The county courts held at Tarvin, on account of the plague.

1605 Thirteen hundred and thirteen died of the plague.— Another admiralty writ refused.

1606 One of the prebendaries in the Cathedral put down the mace carried before the Mayor, which caused much controversy.

1607 Many more soldiers shipped for Ireland under the command of the Earl of Thomond.—Great exertions made to have the Dee causeway removed, in order to prevent the overflow of the meadows, and that the river being scoured, ships might come close to the city.

1608 An assessment levied for repairing the walls.—The plague prevailed, it began at the Talbot.

1614 The city trained band reviewed on the Roodee by Sir George Booth.

1615 Moreton, Bishop of Chester, died. "He was a great scholar and writer against the Papists, but no great housekeeper, and therefore, did not obtain the love of the clergy."

1616 King James came here, August 23rd; he went to the Cathedral, returned by Shoemaker's-row to the Pentice, where he banquetted, and had presented to him a gilt bowl, with 100 jacobuses in it.

1620 An assessment levied for repairing the walls.

1623 This year the races were ordered to be from beyond the
     New Tower round about the Roodee, and a fair cup,
     worth about £8., to be provided yearly by the city.
1627 Eighty pounds levied for repairing the walls.
1630 The Duchess of Tremouille, mother-in-law of Lord Strange,
     arrived here; she was met by the corporation, the artil-
     lery, and at least 600 horsemen.
1633 The aldermen and stewards of the drapers' company com-
     mitted to gaol for unfit speeches against the Mayor,
     until they acknowledged their fault.
1637 Sheriff Wilcock committed to gaol for arresting the goods
     of Robert Green with drawn swords, at his own suit,
     without previous proceedings at law.—Two serjeants-at-
     mace had their gowns taken off.
1639 Newgate repaired.—The Mayor, by order of assembly,
     bound to find, in these perilous times, a corslet and two
     muskets.
1642 First symptoms of civil disturbance broke out in Chester.
     —Charles II. entertained by the corporation at the Pentice.
1645 Siege of Chester took place by the parliamentary forces.
     September 25th, Charles II. marched over Dee bridge
     with 500 horse.
1648 The course of the river ordered to be turned at the
     starting stones.
1649 Colonel Duckinfield appointed governor of Chester.—King
     Charles the Second proclaimed a traitor at the Cross.
1650 The Bishop's palace, with all the furniture, sold for £1059.
1651 On account of the plague at Liverpool, a watch ordered
     to be set at the gates.—A court martial held at Chester,
     and ten individuals found guilty for holding a correspon-
     dence with the King, and executed.
1654 A house of correction ordered to be built.
1657 "All common council men'who had not paid their *haunch
     feasts*, forthwith ordered to pay, or be disfranchised."
1665 Many of the principal gentry of the county sent to the
     castle, under suspicion of being disaffected to Cromwell's
     government.
1678 The city shows entirely abolished.—The first dissenting
     meeting house erected in Chester.
1683 Great outrages committed on the Cathedral, at the insti-
     gation of the Duke of Monmouth.
1687 James the Second came to Chester, was received by the
     corporation, and entertained at the Pentice.
1690 King William visited this city on his way to reduce Ireland.
1691 Ten young women drowned in the Dee, opposite St. John's
     church, by the upsetting of a boat, on Whitsun-Monday.

I 2

1694 A mint being this year set up in Chester, coinage of money began the 2nd of October. There was coined 101,660 ounces of wrought plate; all the pieces had the letter C. under the King's head.

1710 The Roodee enclosed with a cop.

1715 Lord Charles Murray, with several gentlemen, and a great number of private men, who had been taken in the rebellion at Preston, brought prisoners to Chester castle.

1720 Part of the Roodee cop being washed down, was rebuilt, and faced with stone.

1733 First sod of the new cut of the river taken up by R. Manley, Esq. April 20th.

1734 Great contest for the representation of the city, between Sir R. Grosvenor, Bart., and R. Manley, Esq. which lasted seven days, and terminated in favour of the latter.—The act passed incorporating the river Dee company.

1739 Great frost for 13 weeks; carts crossed the river, and a sheep was roasted on the ice.

1745 The Watergate, Northgate, and Sally-ports walled up, and several buildings adjoining the walls pulled down, under apprehension of the Scotch rebels attempting to enter the city.—A number of the rebels brought in 16 carts prisoners to the castle, which being thus filled, the spring assizes were held at Flookersbrook.

1756 The shops on the west side of the Exchange built.

1758 The House of Industry built.

1759 The Infirmary completed.

1762 First police act granted.—St. Peter's spire rebuilt, when one Wright, in attempting to gain the top of the scaffolding, for a trifling wager, fell on the leads of the church, and was killed.

1766 The Newgate enlarged.

1767 First stone of the Eastgate laid on the 8th of August.— The race-ground enlarged, and two stone chairs erected. —Trinity spire struck by lightning; eight yards built for £40.

1770 Trinity church enlarged, and part of the spire rebuilt.

1771 An act passed for making a canal to Nantwich; the first sod cut on the 4th of May.

1772 A horrid explosion of gunpowder in Watergate-street row, on the 5th of November, by which many people lost their lives.

1775 May 2nd, the Chester Chronicle established by Poole and Barker.—22nd, the Cheshire militia, commanded by Earl Cholmondeley, embodied.

1776 April 9th, Rev. J. Wesley preached in the Octagon chapel.

—September 4th, the communication between the canal and the river, near the Water Tower, opened.

1777 January 24th, Dr. Beilby Porteus elected Bishop of Chester.—September, shock of an earthquake felt here.

1778 April 5th, the city huntsman, for a considerable wager, rode his own horse round the walls in $9\frac{1}{2}$ minutes.

1779 March 1st, two Roman hypocausts found in the Linenhall field, about three or four feet under ground.—Aug. 6th, canal between Chester and Nantwich opened for the passage of flats.

1780 February 13th, city illuminated in celebration of Rodney's victory.

1782 May 8. A large fish, 25 ft. long, caught at the Lower Ferry.—Nov. 17. Three felons escaped out of the county gaol.

1783 Feb. 23. The spire of St. Peter's church much damaged by lightning.—May 3. The Cheshire militia arrived in the city.—Musical festival; the receipts exceeded £600.

1784 Jan. 1. A hare, after running through the cathedral, caught in Eastgate-street.—April 16. Contested election for the representation of this city closed: the numbers were, Mr. Grosvenor, 713; Mr. Bootle, 626; Mr. Crewe, 480; and Mr. Barnston, 38.—Cooke, the tragedian, made his first appearance at our theatre.

1785 July 5. The Rev. J. Wesley preached at the Octagon. Sept. 1. Mr. French ascended in Lunardi's balloon, from the Castle-yard, and descended at Macclesfield.—Sept. 7. Mr. Baldwin ascended in his balloon, from the Castle-yard, and descended beyond Warrington.

1786 Feb. 17. St. Bridget's church repaired, and Bridge-street widened.—April 10, 11. Rev. J. Wesley preached in the Octagon chapel.—Aug. 8. Trial respecting the charter took place at Shrewsbury.—Sept. 13. Musical festival for three days.

1787 March 20. The second corporation trial took place at Shrewsbury, the King v. Amery and Monk.—Dec. Dr. Cleaver appointed Bishop of Chester.

1788 March 20. Howard the philanthrophist, in Chester.—June 2. Judgment pronounced in the case of Amery and Monk, for the defendants.—July 3. The old Watergate began to be pulled down.

1789 March 16. The city illuminated in celebration of the king's recovery.—July 14, 15. Mr. Wesley preached in the Octagon chapel.—Sept. 20. Mrs. Jordan performed here.—26. The Dee mills destroyed by fire; loss supposed to be £4000.

1790 April 5. Mr. Wesley preached at the Octagon.—April 19.

Judgment in the case of Amery and Monk reversed by
the House of Lords.—June 13. Lord Belgrave (the late
Marquis of Westminster), elected representative for
Chester, in the room of R. W. Bootle, Esq., who resigned.

1791 June. Cheshire militia embodied ; their parade ground
in the Bottoms-field.—Sept. 6. Grand festival of music.

1793 Jan. 9. Tom Paine burnt in effigy at the Cross.—March
8th, the Cheshire militia left here for Hull.

1794 April, Sir W. W. Wynn's Ancient British regiment of
fencible cavalry raised.

1795 February 13th, death of Thomas Grosvenor, Esq., M.P.
for the city nearly forty years.—15th, death of F. Bower,
Esq., recorder.—June 8th, passage boat launched in the
new canal for the Mersey.

1796 November 10, shock of an earthquake felt in Chester.

1797 October 19, city illuminated in honour of Duncan's
victory.—27th, the Mayor's feast abolished by Rowland
Jones, Mayor.

1798 March 15, the voluntary subscription in Chester, for the
defence of the country, amounted to £6214.—July 21,
death of Hon. Sergeant Adair, Chief Justice of Chester.
—October 4, the city illuminated, in consequence of
Nelson's victory of the Nile.

1799 July 13, Sir William Grant resigned the office of Chief
Justice of Chester.—Novem. 7, Ancient British Fencibles
arrived here, preparatory to their being disbanded.

1800 April 2, Dr. Majendie appointed Bishop of Chester.

1801 June 1, shock of an earthquaite felt here about 2 A.M.,
in direction from north to south.—Aug. 2, dreadful storm
of thunder, lightning, and rain.—Oct. 11, City illuminated in consequence of the peace.—Nov. 30, alarm of fire
at the theatre ; a great number of people severely bruised.

1802 Jan. 21, dreadful storm of wind. The vanes blown off
the churches, and several houses unroofed. The militia
and volunteers disbanded this year.—July 6, Lord Belgrave and General Grosvenor elected members for the
city.—Aug. 5, death of Earl Grosvenor, the oldest alderman of the corporation.—25, first court held by the mayor
in the exchange after taking down the pentice at the cross.

1803 April 4, the militia called out and assembled at the castle.
—Volunteer corps raised, and inspected on the Roodee
by the Duke of Gloucester.—Sept. 5, a cask, containing
coins of William III. to the amount of £800, found near
Parkgate. King William's army encamped there, on its
way to Ireland.—£3500 raised by the corporation and
citizens of Chester for clothing the volunteers.—Dec. 28,

a rupture between the press-gang and the volunteers.— The Northgate broken open, and a prisoner liberated.

1804 Feb. 7. Volunteers inspected by Col. Cuyler; they mustered 1266, and in June marched to Oswestry and Ellesmere.—Aug. 24. Trial of the volunteers for the tumult with the press-gang; Dan. Humphreys found guilty.

1805 Jan. 8. Parry and Truss's coach manufactory burnt down. —May 15. The volunteers marched to Warrington for 21 days' permanent duty.—Nov. 9. City illuminated in consequence of Nelson's victory.—Dec. 10. Death of Dean Cotton, at Bath.

1806 Jan. 25. Rev. Hugh Cholmondeley appointed Dean.— March 4. Old buildings at the Cross pulled down.—July 28. Dreadful storm; the mast of a ship at the Crane shivered to pieces by lightning.—Sept. 24. Loss of the 'King George' packet, off Hoylake, in this port, with 170 passengers on board; only four sailors and the steward saved.—Sept. 30. Festival of music.—Oct. 31. General Grosvenor and Mr. Drax Grosvenor returned as members for the city.—Nov. 25. Snuff-mills destroyed by fire.

1807 May 6. Mr. John Egerton elected member of parliament. —Dec. 15. Grand dinner given by Mr. Egerton to the officers of the volunteers, at Oulton.

1808 Nov. Chester local militia established.—Nov. 20. Disturbance at the theatre, in opposition to the song of the 'Sixth of May' being sung.

1809 Jan. 13. The sugar-house in Cuppin-lane destroyed by fire.—May 4. Chester local militia first assembled.— July 5. Union Hall, Foregate-street, first opened.—Oct. Dr. F. B. Sparkes elected Bishop of Chester. Oct. 25. Celebration of the jubilee of King George III.

1810 Aug. 22. Prince of Orange in Chester.—Sept. 22. Rioters in the theatre all found guilty.—Nov. 9. Piece of plate, value 150 guineas, presented by the officers of the local militia, to Colonel Barnstone

1811 March 24. Scaffolding erected for taking down the spire of Trinity church.—Sept. Portraits of Earl Grosvenor and his noble father presented to the corporation, and placed in the council-chamber.—Dec. 5. Parry and Truss's coach manufactory burnt down a second time.

1812 Application for a mandamus against the mayor refused by the court of King's Bench.—April. Great number of Luddites brought to the castle.—June 23. Arrival of Dr. Law, the new bishop.—Oct. 8. Great contest for the city representation, which lasted 11 days. General Grosvenor and Mr. Egerton returned.

1813 Nov. 5. The mayor, Sir W. W. Wynn, gave a magnificent entertainment to above 200 persons.—Dec. Mrs. Jordan performed at the theatre.

1814 June 17. The city illuminated in commemoration of general peace.—July 7. General thanksgiving for peace ; the corporation and other public bodies went in procession to the cathedral.—Aug. 15. Grand fête given to Lords Combermere and Hill, for their services in the wars.—Sept. 26. Festival of music ; principal singers, Braham and Catalini.—Nov. St. Mary's church-yard inclosed with iron railing.

1815 April 23. Kean's first appearance at the Chester theatre.—Sept. 23. Earl of Chester's legion of yeomanry cavalry, commanded by Sir J. F. Leicester, Bart., on duty here.

1816 March. Anne Moore, the celebrated *fasting* woman, confined in the castle, for a robbery at Stockport; during her confinement she *miraculously* recovered her appetite.—May 24. Rope warehouse on the Roodee destroyed by fire.—July 4. The mayor, J. Cotgreave, Esq., received the honour of knighthood.

1817 Jan. 4. The Grand Duke Nicholas of Russia, who had been making a tour of the northern part of England, visited Chester.—March 13. Twenty-one men, charged with treasonable practices at Heaton Norris, committed to the castle.—June 3. Fire in the ship-yard of Mr. Courtney, near the Crane.—Oct. 20. A savings' bank established in Chester.—Nov. 19. Being the day appointed for the funeral of the Princess Charlotte, the shops were closed, and all business suspended.

1818 Election of members of parliament for the city. Lord Belgrave and General Grosvenor returned.

1819 Jan. Gas-lights introduced into the streets.—March 6. Dreadful fire at the Dee mills; the whole fabric, with its contents, consumed, and one life lost ; the loss estimated at £40,000.—Oct. 16. Prince Leopold, consort of the Princess Charlotte, presented with the freedom of the city.

1820 June 16. The court of King's Bench granted a rule for a criminal information against Mr. Williamson, the late mayor, for refusing to admit several individuals to their freedom during the late election.—Dec The Duke of Wellington entertained at the Exchange ; Lords Combermere, Hill, and Kenyon, Sir W. W. Wynn, and a number of other distinguished individuals were present.

1821 Jan. 13. Fire broke out at the Leadworks.—June 11. Coronation of George IV. celebrated.—Sept. 25. Grand festival of music.—Oct. Two mayors, and two sets of aldermen and common councilmen chosen; the opposition party were subsequently ousted.

1822 March 31.   S. Y. Benyon, Esq., recorder, died.—June 29.   The steam-boiler belonging to Mr. Boult, tobacco-manufacturer, in Cuppin-street, burst.   The explosion was terrific; a considerable portion of the premises were laid in ruins, and the windows of the adjoining houses shattered.   Mr. Boult and three of his men were so dreadfully injured that they all died in a few days afterwards.—

1823 Feb. 24.   The coach manufactory of Mr. Parry, in Fore-gate-street, *for the third time*, with all its contents, completely destroyed by fire.—April 26.   Great rejoicings in the city on the birth of a son to Lord Belgrave.—Sept. 30.   The coming of age of R. H. Barnston, son and heir of Colonel Barnston, celebrated with great rejoicings.

1824 June 7.   Mr. Sadler ascended in his balloon from the Castle-yard, and descended near Utkinton.—Sept. 2.   The coach manufactory of Mr. Parry, for the *fourth time* destroyed by fire.

1825 June.   The act for erecting the new bridge over the Dee, &c. passed both houses of parliament.

1826 May.   The water-works bill this month passed through both houses of parliament.—June.   Contested election for representation; Lord Belgrave and the Hon. Robert Grosvenor were the successful candidates.

1827 Oct.   First stone of the new bridge laid by the late Marquis of Westminster, attended by the bishop, clergy, the corporation, and a vast number of citizens.

1828 July 24 and 25.   Excessive fall of rain and hail, which did immense injury to the city and neighbourhood.   About 15 yards of the city walls, between the Abbey-street and the Phœnix Tower, fell down.—Sept. 30.   A dreadful fire in the oil and drug warehouse of Mr. Thos. Bowers, in Northgate-street.

1829 Sept.   Splendid musical festival and fancy dress ball.

1831 May 6.   The Hon. R. Grosvenor and Mr. Cunliffe Offley elected members for the city.—17.   Lord Viscount Belgrave and Mr. Wilbraham returned as members of the county.—Sept. 8.   The coronation of King William and Queen Adelaide celebrated with great festivity.—Nov. 8.   A board of health established, in consequence of the prevalence of the cholera.

1832 Jan. 7.   Paganini at the theatre.—April 18.   Cunliffe Offley, Esq., M.P. for the city, died.—May 14.   J. F. Maddock, Esq. elected as representative, in the place of the deceased Mr. Offley.—June 29.   The cholera morbus prevalent.—July 28.   A smart shock of earthquake felt in this neighbourhood.   The cholera entirely disappears.— Oct. 14.   The Duchess of Kent and the Princess Victoria visit Eaton Hall.—16.   Their Royal Highnesses visit the city.—Nov. 12.   The Duke of Sussex visits Eaton Hall. —13.   Visits Chester, and is presented with the freedom of the city.—Dec. 9.   Lord Grosvenor and Mr. Jervis elected representatives of the city.

1833 Nov. 20.   A dreadful gale of wind; great damage done in the city and surrounding neighbourhood.—Dec. 31.   Terrific hurricane.   The river rose to an unprecedented height.

1834 June 8.   A remarkable fish, the " Squalus Vulgaris," or angel fish, caught off Connah's Quay.—Sept. 9.   The first stone of Pepper-street chapel laid.—14.   Messrs. Frost's steam-mills burnt down; the loss estimated at £6,000.

1835 June 1.   A military sham fight on the Roodee.

1836 Feb. 7.   John Cottingham, Esq., elected recorder.—Dec 16.   Presentation of plate to Geo. Harrison, Esq., late mayor.·

1837 Feb. 10.   Death of Colonel Roger Barnston.—March 21. Great rejoicings in celebration of the 70th anniversary of the Marquis of Westminster's birth-day.—June 30.   Cere- mony of laying the first stone of Christ's Church in New- town.   Proclamation of Queen Victoria.

1838 March 30.   Splendid new lodge erected by the late Mar- quis of Westminster, at Overleigh.   This lodge is a copy of the gate of St. Augustine, at Canterbury.—April 13. The new barracks in the upper ward completed.   This building affords accommodation for 400 infantry.—April 20.   The Water Tower, granted to the Mechanics' Insti- tution as a museum, &c., opened to the public.—June 28.   The coronation of Queen Victoria celebrated with great rejoicings.—Aug. 22.   Monument erected to Colonel Barnston in the cathedral.—Oct. 20.   The organ used at the coronation of Her Majesty in Westminster Abbey, erected in St. John's church.

1839 Jan. 6.   Dreadful hurricane; part of a buttress of the tower of the cathedral fell and broke through the roof of the north transept.   Twenty to thirty yards of the bound- ary wall of the city gaol demolished.   The windows of St. John's church nearly all shattered.   The building for- merly used as a soapery in Grosvenor-street, totally ruined; destruction of property estimated at £10,000. March 29.   An ancient crypt discovered on the west side of Bridge-street, and excavated.   The style of archi- tecture is of the eleventh century, and the foundation is in the solid rock.

1840 July 22. A fire broke out in the morning on the premises of Messrs. Caldecott, hatters and drapers, and destroyed stock to the amount of £3,000. Two Ashantee princes visited Chester and Eaton.—Sept. 23. Chester and Birkenhead railway opened for public conveyance.—Oct. 1. Chester and Crewe railway opened.

1841 June 4. W. N. Welsby, Esq. nominated recorder.

1842 Sept. 1. The Chester Training College opened.—Oct. 18. Post-office business removed to premises in St. John-street.

1843 Severe shocks of an earthquake felt at Chester and in Lancashire.—Oct. Autumn race meeting established.

1844 July 11. The King of Saxony visited Chester on a tour through England.—Aug. First exhibition at the Mechanics' Institution.

1845 Jan. 2. Destructive fire at Mr. Mulvey's ship-yard.— Feb. 17. Marquis of Westminster died in the 78th year of his age. On the day of the funeral the shops were closed and business partially suspended, in respect to the deceased nobleman.

1846 May. Thirty-one horses started for the Tradesmen's Cup, which was won by Mr. G. H. Moore's "Coranna;" value of the stakes after all deductions, £2,040.

1847 Jan. 22. Destructive fire at the Dee mills, the whole of one mill destroyed.—May 24. Accident at the Dee railway bridge; one of the outside girders on the Saltney side having broken as the quarter to six train p.m. passed over. Four people were killed on the spot, and several severely injured.

1848 Chester and Holyhead railway opened to Bangor.—Oct. Shrewsbury and Chester railway opened throughout.

1849 Foundation stone laid of the new tower of St. Michael's church.

1850 The Hon. W. O. Stanley, M.P., elected representative for the city, in the place of Sir John Jervis, promoted to the Lord Chief Justiceship. Chester and Holyhead Railway opened throughout.

1851 A dreadful accident took place in the Sutton Tunnel of the Lancashire and Cheshire Junction Railway, on the Chester Cup day; several lives were lost, and many persons seriously injured.

THE GENERAL RAILWAY STATION

Is situated in Flookersbrook, and is the terminus of six different lines of railway, viz., the London and North Western, the Chester and Holyhead, the Chester and Mold, the Birkenhead, Lancashire, and Cheshire Junction, the Chester and Birkenhead, and the Shrewsbury and Chester, four of which companies contributed in rateable proportions towards the erection of the building. It is one of the most extensive railway establishments in the kingdom, and the works comprise a large and elegant passenger and arrival shed, with all suitable offices, and adjoining which is a most commodious spare carriage shed, a goods depôt, gas works, water works, and three engine sheds. The whole was designed by C. H. Wild, Esq. C. E., and Mr. Thompson, of London, and carried out under the supervision of Robert Stephenson, Esq. C.E., M.P.

The Passenger Shed occupies a space of ground nearly a quarter of a mile in length, and presents to the city an elegant façade 1010 feet long, or a frontage, including the house and carriage landings, of 1160 feet. It is built of dark coloured bricks, relieved with copings and facings of Stourton stone. At each end of the station and projecting from the main building, there is a shed for the arrival of trains, each 290 feet long by 24 feet broad, covered with an iron roof; in these sheds cabs and omnibuses await the arrival of all trains.

On the inner side of the building is the General Departure Platform, extending 740 feet in length by 20 feet in width; this and three lines of rails is covered with an exceedingly chaste and elegant iron roof of 60 feet span, designed and carried out by C. H. Wild, Esq. C.E. Behind this shed again, but visible from the general platform through the arches, is the spare carriage shed, 600 feet long by 52 feet broad. The whole arrangements of the buildings are admirably adapted to carry on with comfort to the public and with facility to the employées, the immense business that has so suddenly been brought to the city by the convergence of so many railways at this point.

Some idea may be formed of the extent of the business here transacted, when it is stated that of passenger trains only, there now arrive and depart upwards of 80 trains, averaging 2,000 passengers daily. The number of passengers who took tickets at Chester station during the year 1850 was 400,000.

The Goods Depôt is situated immediately behind the passengers' building, and fully accords with it in style. It consists of a shed 180 feet long and 120 feet wide, with four railway entrances; and containing three platforms or decks, furnished with 18 cranes and light weighing machines, and the wagons are run alongside the decks to receive or discharge their loads.

There are about 40 goods, cattle, and mineral trains to receive and forward every day; and during the year 1850 380,000 tons of merchandize passed through manipulation at this station, giving a daily average of more than 1000 tons— a singular contrast to the traffic of some few years back, when railways were in their infancy, and a solitary goods wagon was found ample for the conveyance of all goods along the London and North Western line consigned to Chester.

The Gas and Water Works were erected in consequence of the unreasonable demand made by the public companies for the supply of these two essentials, and it is understood that the station committee have every reason to congratulate themselves upon the steps they took.

The works are quite in character with the other buildings. The gas works are fitted up with twelve retorts, and deliver annually about six million cubic feet, the consumption being large from the fact of all the pointsmen's huts being heated by means of gas-stoves; and the cleanliness, comfort, and order of the huts bear a most favourable contrast with those of other lines or stations where coal is used as the stove fuel. The cost of gas to the committee does not, we understand, exceed 2s. 6d. per 1000 cubic feet.

The Water Works adjoin the gas works, and are supplied from a beautiful and plentiful spring at Christleton, from whence it is brought along the line to the station reservoir, and from thence pumped at the rate of 500 gallons per minute into a tank on the top of the building, which is sufficiently elevated to ensure a continuous supply to all the upper stories of the general station.

The extent of land purchased by the general station committee for station purposes is about 75 acres; and within the station precincts there is upwards of 7 miles of railway line, with 51 turn-tables. The gross cost of the land and buildings has been about £240,000.

The affairs of the station are watched over by a committee of eight gentlemen, who are elected from the boards of the four contributing companies, and their views are carried out by their manager and secretary, R. L. Jones, Esq., who has so well organised his large staff of officers and men that the arduous and responsible duties devolving upon him in his double capacity of passenger and goods manager are performed, not only with the greatest efficiency, but also with a most satisfactory courtesy and convenience to the public.

CAB FARES.

Not exceeding three persons; to or from the Railway Station in Brook-street—from or to any part of the city, within the point where the Whitchurch and Northwich roads turn off—Abbot's Grange and the College—the Sluice House, including Crane-street and Paradise-row—the May-Pole in Handbridge and the New Bridge toll-house, *One Shilling.* The same distance; four persons, *One Shilling and Sixpence.* Any distance beyond the Borough, *One Shilling* per mile. No gratuities allowed to be demanded by the drivers of any cars plying within the Borough boundary, and no charge to be made for luggage not exceeding 100lbs in weight.

FARES TO OR FROM ANY OTHER PART OF THE CITY.

Not exceeding three persons; any distance not exceeding 1 mile, *One Shilling;* and at the rate of *One Shilling* per mile for every additional mile; and *Sixpence* for every additional half-mile or fractional part of half-a-mile. For four persons; any distance not exceeding 1 mile, *One Shilling and Sixpence.* For four persons; any distance exceeding 1 mile, and not exceeding 2 miles, *Two Shillings.* For four persons, any distance exceeding 2 miles, at the rate of *Two Shillings* for the first mile, and *One Shilling* per mile for every additional mile, and *Sixpence* for every additional half-mile or fractional part of half-a-mile.

BY TIME.

Not exceeding one hour, *Two Shillings and Sixpence;* and *Sixpence* for every fifteen minutes and fractional part of fifteen minutes beyond the hour. In all cases it shall be at the option of the owner or driver to charge by time or distance.

THE POPULATION OF CHESTER.

According to the Census, taken March 31st, 1851, the following is a statement of the population of each parish.

PARISHES OF	MALES.	FEMALES.	TOTAL.
St. Oswald	3243	3430	6673
St. Peter	430	518	948
St. Bridget	360	501	861
St. Martin	232	304	536
Trinity	1499	1875	3374
Little St. John's Hospital	39	12	51
Cathedral precincts	145	232	377
St. John	3995	4492	8487
St. Mary	1620	1688	3308
St. Michael	346	429	775
St. Olave	265	253	518
Township of Great Boughton (Borough portion)	445	514	959
Spittal Boughton	69	89	158
Chester Castle	507	84	591

POPULATION OF CHESTER IN

1811	17472	1841	23375
1821	19949	1851	27616
1831	21373		

DISTANCES FROM TOWN TO TOWN IN THE COUNTY OF CHESTER.

The names of the respective Towns are on the top and side, and the square where both meet gives the distance.

Distance from London.

	Altringham																	180
Chester	31	Chester																182
Congleton	21	33	Congleton															162
Frodsham	24	10	29	Frodsham														192
Knutsford	7	25	14	17	Knutsford													176
Macclesfield	16	38	9	28	12	Macclesfield												167
Malpas	37	15	30	24	33	35	Malpas											169
Middlewich	16	20	13	18	9	18	24	Middlewich										167
Mottram	17	48	25	40	22	16	51	31	Mottram									187
Nantwich	28	20	18	24	21	23	12	12	43	Nantwich								164
Northwich	13	18	19	12	7	20	26	6	30	17	Northwich							174
Parkgate	36	10	42	16	31	45	26	30	53	30	28	Parkgate						190
Runcorn	24	15	36	6	16	28	30	20	41	27	14	20	Runcorn					188
Sandbach	19	25	9	23	11	17	22	5	41	10	11	35	25	Sandbach				162
Stockport	9	40	20	33	14	12	44	23	8	35	22	45	33	25	Stockport			179
Tarporley	25	10	25	15	19	26	14	10	42	9	12	20	16	15	34	Tarporley		172
Tarvin	25	6	27	10	19	32	18	14	42	14	12	16	12	19	34	4	Tarvin	178

HOTELS.

The principal hotels in Chester are—the Royal at the Eastgate, and the Albion in Lower Bridge-street; the Green Dragon in Eastgate-street, the Feathers in Bridge-street, the Blossoms and the Hop-pole in Foregate-street, the White Lion in Northgate-street, besides many others of very good repute.

CHESTER COUNTY COURT.

OFFICE.—Watergate Street. Attendance from 10 to 4. JUDGE.—J. W. Harden, Esq. TREASURER.—John Trevor, Esq. CLERK OF THE COURT.—Hugh Wallace, Esquire, Solicitor. ASSISTANT CLERK.—Mr. J. Rogers. HIGH BAILIFF.—Mr. Wm. Knott. BAILIFF.—Mr. John Pickering. BROKER.—Mr. Wm. Fox.

ERRATA.

Page 49—for " Cemetry," read " Cemetery."
 ,,   65—for " as in weather," read " as in *wet* weather."
 ,,   88—for " Thucydedes," read "Thucydides."
 ,,   89—for " Dean Swift," read " Dean Smith."
 ,,   90—for " beautiful design by Mr. Massey," read " Mr. Hussey."

INDEX.

K

G. PRICHARD, BRIDGE STREET ROW, CHESTER.

WILLIAM HEATH,

(SUCCESSOR TO W. SPRENT,)

GROCER, TEA DEALER, & PERFUMER,

EASTGATE STREET ROW,

CHESTER.

FOR ITS PURITY,

FOR its Medicinal qualities, and high Testimonials from the Faculty for its safe and efficacious effect in all cases of diarrhœa, as a preventative against Cholera, combined with its immense increase of consumption during the test of many years' agency in this city, it is that

W. HEATH,

Strongly recommends BETTS & CO.'s PATENT BRANDY, at 16s. per gallon in draught, or 36s. per dozen bottles, pale or coloured.

GIN.

The following Testimonial is sufficient proof of the vast superiority in purity of flavour, and all other respects, of MESSRS. BETTS AND CO.'S PATENT GIN :—

MESSRS. BETTS AND Co.—Having examined the Spirit with which you prepare your Patent Gin, and also the ingredients with which it is flavoured, and having witnessed the whole process of its distillation and preparation, I am prepared to state that it contains no deleterious matter whatever, and that the non-existence of various prejudicial ingredients, commonly employed in the manufacture of Gin, in my opinion gives yours a decided preference

JOHN THOMAS COOPER,
Professor of Chemistry.

Sold at 12s. 6d per gallon, and 26s. per dozen, bottles included.

THE DEW OF BEN NEVIS.

GATHERINGS OF LONG JOHN,

The celebrated Highland Distiller to his Royal Highness Prince Albert and the Prince of Wales.

Sold in bottles, secured with Capsules, by the sole Consignees, 42s. per dozen, bottles included.

FINE OLD COGNAC BRANDY................ 24s. 0d. per gallon.
OLD JAMAICA RUM .... 14s. 6d.   ,,
OLD MALT WHISKEY........................ 16s. 6d.   ,,
BRITISH WINES ... . 14s. 0d. per dozen.

W. HEATH,

(SUCCESSOR TO W. SPRENT.)

Begs to offer the above pure Spirits to Famlies at his GROCERY AND ITALIAN WAREHOUSE,

EASTGATE ROW, CHESTER.

MRS. CHEERS,
STAY MANUFACTURER,
Baby Linen and Juvenile Repository,
EASTGATE ROW,
CHESTER.

FRANCIS F. HICKMAN,
(Many years with Messrs. Walker and Peters),

Manufacturer of

ALL KINDS OF COPPER, ZINC, AND TIN WARE.

LAMP AND BATH WAREHOUSE,

FURNISHING IRONMONGER
AND CUTLER.

145, NORTHGATE-STREET, CHESTER.

COPPER GOODS TINNED AND REPAIRS NEATLY EXECUTED.

WILLIAMS, JONES & WILLIAMS,
Tobacco and Snuff Manufacturers,
CHESTER.

JAMES HOLAWAY,

(Upwards of 46 years in the employ of the late firm of Messrs. Parry and Son),

WHOLESALE AND RETAIL

BRUSH MANUFACTURER,
NORTHGATE·STREET,
CHESTER,

J. G. SHAW,

157, BRIDGE STREET, CROSS, CHESTER,

IRONMONGER, BRAZIER, & CUTLER,

MANUFACTURER OF

TIN, COPPER, AND IRON GOODS,

GAS-FITTER AND BELL-HANGER.

A great variety of

Patent and other Dining and Drawing-room

REGISTER GRATES.
KITCHEN RANGES,

With back Boilers, Stoves, and all the recent improvements. Bed-room Grates, and Sham Registers. Patent

WROUGHT-IRON BEDSTEADS.

The newest Designs in

BRONZED AND STEEL FENDERS
AND FIRE-IRONS.

Japanned Coal Vases, &c. Hip, Shower, and Sponging
Baths. Master's and Kent's Patent Knife-Cleaning
Machines. Papier Machée and Japanned Trays. Bronzed
Tea Urns, Swing Kettles. Every variety of Gas-fittings
and Chandeliers. Copper Pans, &c. Tinned and Re-
paired. Brass-work Bronzed and Lacquered.

Agricultural and Garden Implements ; Scales, Weights
and Measures, and Weighing Machines; Cast Iron
Eaves, Troughs, Down Piping, and every variety of
Iron Work for Building and other purposes.

Plate Powder, Polishing Paste, and Black Lead ;
Adams's Patent Composition for Polishing Furniture.

W. ROBINSON,

FEATHER'S HOTEL & COMMERCIAL INN,

BRIDGE STREET, CHESTER.

SUPERIOR ACCOMMODATION FOR VISITORS AND FAMILIES.

NEAT CARS, GIGS, ETC.

WOOLLEN DRAPERY ESTABLISHMENT.

JOHN AND THOMAS HIGGINS,

14, BRIDGE-STREET ROW,

Have always on hand a large assortment of Goods in the above line of Business, with a great variety of RAILWAY RUGS, CARPET BAGS, SHIRTS, SHIRT FRONTS, SHIRT COLLARS, BRACES, UMBRELLAS, GLOVES,

HATS, BOYS' CAPS, &c.

To which they beg to call the attention of the Public, whose patronage they respectfully solicit.

FUNERALS FURNISHED.

EDWARD NOYES,

CARVER AND GILDER

AND

PLATE GLASS WAREHOUSE,

26, *Bridge-Street Row, Chester,*

Returns his grateful thanks to his numerous Friends and the Public for the distinguished support he continues to receive, and respectfully begs leave to inform them that he manufactures all kind of Modern and Antique Portrait Frames. Chimney and Pier Glasses made to order in the most fashionable style, and on moderate terms; and House Gilding in all its branches.

W. S. BEVIN,

WOOLLEN DRAPER AND TAILOR,

EASTGATE STREET,

CHESTER.

FUNERALS COMPLETELY FURNISHED.

JAMES ROGERS,

ACCOUNTANT,

LAW STATIONER, & ESTATE AGENT,

(Agent to the Minerva Life and District Fire Insurance Company,)

5, WHITE FRIARS,

CHESTER.

ELIZABETH BELL,

HOP-POLE,

COMMERCIAL AND FAMILY INN,

FOREGATE STREET,

CHESTER.

GEORGE MARSH,

WOOLLEN DRAPER AND TAILOR,

5, *BRIDGE STREET ROW*,

CHESTER.

Funerals Furnished.

G. M. solicits a trial to prove the advantages of ready money ; small profits and a quick return being the order of the day.

J. KEARTLAND,

WHOLESALE AND RETAIL

TEA DEALER AND GROCER,

140, Upper Bridge-Street,

CHESTER.

PLATT AND SON,

Chemists in ordinary to Her Majesty,

13, FOREGATE-STREET, CHESTER.

IMPORTERS & DEALERS IN GERMAN & FRENCH PERFUMERY
Medicinal Waters, &c.

Also every article of utility and fashion required in a Chemist's business.

WHALEY'S

FAMILY HOTEL & POSTING HOUSE,

ALBION HOTEL, CHESTER.

SUPERIOR STABLING WITH LOCK-UP COACH-HOUSES.

Conveyances to and from the Railway.

ALEX. & WM. BOOTH,

HAT MANUFACTURERS

AND

MERCHANT CLOTHIERS,

99, *EASTGATE STREET, CHESTER.*

WHOLESALE WAREHOUSES NEAR THE CATHEDRAL.

W. W. BRITTAIN,

Bridge Street Row,

CLOTHIER AND HATTER.

FUNERALS FURNISHED.

ORIGINAL BAZAAR,

No. 36, BRIDGE - STREET ROW, CHESTER.

PIETRO BORDESSA,

Manufacturer of Weather Glasses, &c.

Dealer in Fancy Toys, Foreign Fancy Merchandise, Jewellery,
Gilt Toys.

Magnetic Rings, Dressing Cases, Writing Desks, Work Boxes.

CLOTHES, TOOTH, NAIL, AND HAIR BRUSHES.

A VARIETY OF BERLIN, FRENCH, DUTCH, & GERMAN BASKETS.

BAROMETERS & THERMOMETERS SOLD & REPAIRED.

Importer of Naples Macaroni direct.

N.B. PLEASE OBSERVE—REMOVED TO No. 36, BRIDGE-ST. ROW.

W. HIGGINS,

DISPENSING CHEMIST,

142, *BRIDGE STREET (WEST),*

CHESTER.

In preparing Prescriptions, the strictest care is paid to Accuracy, and to the Purity of the Medicines.

POWELL AND EDWARDS,

CUTLERS & IRONMONGERS,

BRIDGE STREET.

S. DAVIES,
PHARMACEUTICAL CHEMIST,
12, BRIDGE STREET ROW,
CHESTER.

JOHN FIELDING,
GLASS, CHINA, AND STAFFORDSHIRE
WAREHOUSE,

145, Upper Bridge Street,

CHESTER.

PETER HILTON,

White Lion Hotel & Commercial Inn,
NORTHGATE-STREET, CHESTER.

CARS TO AND FROM THE RAILWAY STATION.

JOHN LLOYD,
Dispensing Chemist and Tea Dealer,
EASTGATE-STREET,
(Near the Cross,) Chester.

Prescriptions carefully prepared, under the immediate care of the Principal, and with Medicines of the purest quality.—PATENT MEDICINES.

N.B. Agent to the British Hong Kong Tea Company.
       ,,   Twelvetree's Washing Liquid.
       ,,   Silkes's English Revelenta.

CLAYTON, SHUTTLEWORTH, & CO.,

STAMP END WORKS, LINCOLN,

AND

78, LOMBARD STREET, LONDON, E.C.

IMPROVED PORTABLE STEAM ENGINES.

The large and increasing demand for CLAYTON, SHUTTLEWORTH, & CO.'S Steam Engines and Machinery, together with the numerous and flattering testimonials daily received, is a sufficient proof of the high estimation in which they are held, both in this and foreign countries, and renders it quite unnecessary to say much upon the subject in an Advertisement. *Already more than two thousand seven hundred have been manufactured,* upwards of five hundred of which, of various powers, were disposed of within the last twelve months. Simplicity of construction, combined with correct principles, excellence of workmanship, and quality of materials, are the aim of CLAYTON, SHUTTLEWORTH, & CO., in all their manufactures.

Full particulars, in Illustrated Catalogues, on application.

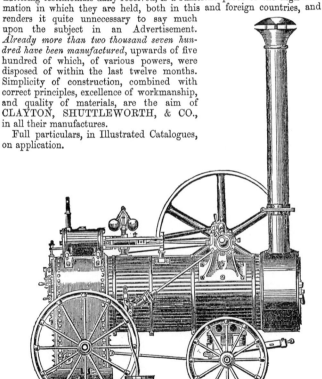

The above may be seen in the Show-yard of the

SMITH AND ASHBY,

𝔄gricultural 𝔍mplement 𝔐anufacturers,

STAMFORD, LINCOLNSHIRE,

Beg to direct attention to their celebrated **HAYMAKING MACHINES,** Patent Steel Tooth **HORSE RAKES,** Patent Wheel **HAND RAKES,** New Patent Improved **CHAFF-CUTTING MACHINES,** Oil Cake Mills, and Horse Works, They also invite special notice of their New **TWO-AND-A-HALF HORSE PORTABLE STEAM ENGINE,** for agricultural and general use, with compact Thrashing Machine, Grinding Mill, Chaff Cutter, Root Pulper, Cake Mill, Corn Crusher, and Circular Saw Bench to attach to ditto. Now exhibiting at their stand, No. 27, in the Show-yard.

SMITH & ASHBY'S ORIGINAL PATENT HAYMAKER.

This is the Machine that took the £5 prize against Mr. Nicholson's Haymaker, at the GREAT WATERFORD TRIAL, last August (1857), immediately after the Salisbury Show. The above trial was conducted under the direction of the same Judge who was engaged at the Royal Society's Trials at Salisbury. The circumstance proves that Smith and Ashby's Machine is the best Haymaker in use. This celebrated Machine has taken Thirty-one First-class Prizes, and has stood the test of twelve years.

N.B.—S. & A. are now constructing all their Haymakers on their original patent principle, and exactly like the one that took the Prize at Waterford; and they warrant every Machine they send out. Price £15 15s.

☞ **Smith & Ashby's Haymaker has just taken the Prize of the Royal Bath and West of England Society, at Cardiff.**

FIXED STEAM ENGINE.

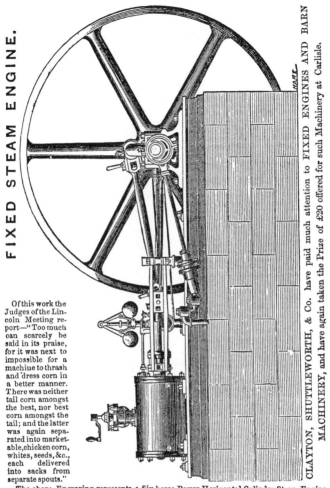

CLAYTON, SHUTTLEWORTH, & Co. have paid much attention to FIXED ENGINES AND BARN MACHINERY, and have again taken the Prize of £20 offered for such Machinery at Carlisle.

Of this work the Judges of the Lincoln Meeting report—"Too much can scarcely be said in its praise, for it was next to impossible for a machine to thrash and dress corn in a better manner. There was neither tail corn amongst the best, nor best corn amongst the tail; and the latter was again separated into marketable, chicken corn, whites, seeds, &c., each delivered into sacks from separate spouts."

The above Engraving represents a Six-horse Power Horizontal Cylinder Steam Engine, erected complete upon metal foundation plate, which arrangement renders it easy of removal —an important point to a Tenant Farmer. The principle of this Engine is direct action, which simplifies the whole arrangement, inasmuch as the working parts are fewer in number, more compact, and less likely to get out of repair. Being secured upon one bedplate renders it unnecessary to have any bearings or fastenings in the partition or adjoining walls of the building in which it is inclosed.

It is supplied with Cylindrical Cornish Boiler of ample size and strength, the whole being made of the very best material, fitted and finished in a style equal to any house in the trade.

N.B.—As different situations, in almost every case, involve special arrangements, C., S., & Co. will be happy to furnish Plans and Specifications where fixed machinery is required.

The above may be seen in the Show-yard of the

PORTABLE GRINDING MILL.

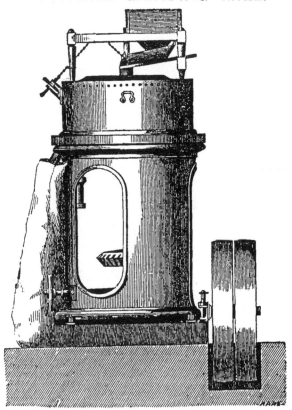

CLAYTON, SHUTTLEWORTH, & CO.

Call attention to their GRINDING MILL, which has taken the Prize
year after year; also, Sawing Machinery, Irrigating Machinery, to be driven
by their Portable Engines, &c., &c., particulars of which, in an Illustrated
Catalogue, will be forwarded free, on application to the

STAMP END WORKS, LINCOLN.

OR

78, LOMBARD STREET, LONDON, E.C.

Royal Agricultural Society, Chester Meeting.

JOHN WARNER AND SONS,

Hydraulic Engineers, and Bell and Brass Founders to Her Majesty,

8, CRESCENT, CRIPPLEGATE, LONDON;

And at the Royal Agricultural Society's Show at Chester, where the following and many other articles may be seen at their stand.

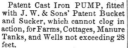

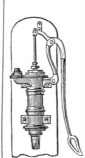

Patent Cast Iron PUMP, fitted with J. W. & Sons' Patent Bucket and Sucker, which cannot clog in action, for Farms, Cottages, Manure Tanks, and Wells not exceeding 28 feet.

Dia.	Height.	£	s.
2½ in. short, 1 ft. 7 in.	......	1	10
2½ in. long, 3 „ 3 „	......	1	14
3 „ 3 „ 6 „	......	2	8
3½ „ 3 „ 6 „	......	2	12
4 „ 3 „ 6 „	......	3	3
2½ in. short, with 15 ft. of Lead Pipe attached, ready for fixing	......	2	14
2½ in. long, do., do.	......	2	18

Patent Brass LIFT and FORCE PUMP, on Plank, for House purposes, supply of Cisterns, &c.

Dia.	£	s.
2½ inch	......	6	0
3 „	......	7	5
3½ „	......	8	0

A lighter Pump, of 3 inches diameter, can be supplied, if required, at 5 15

IMPROVED LIQUID MANURE, OR GENERAL PORTABLE PUMP.

These Pumps are fitted with J. W. & Sons' Patent Bucket and Sucker, and cannot clog in action. The Barrel is of Galvanized Iron, not likely to corrode, and can be raised or lowered at pleasure. The Legs will fold together, and the whole may be carried on the shoulder to any pond or tank required.

Larger sizes of the above, if required.

Price of 4½ in. Liquid Manure Pump, with legs, £3 3s.; 1¾ in. Gutta Percha Suction Pipe, 1s. 11d. per foot; 2 in. Flexible Rubber and Canvas Suction Pipe, 3s. per foot. The Barrel is 27¾ inches long, and the legs are 5 feet high.

BRASS SYRINGES, from 9s. to 18s.

CONSERVATORY PUMP, No. 32, with Warner's Registered Spreader, 27s. 6d.

Warner's Cattle and Sheep Bells, in Sets of 6, with straps, per set, 13s.

Musical Sheep Bells, with straps, in sets of 6, 19s.; ditto, in sets of 8, 25s.; ditto, in sets of 12, 38s.

The great 16-ton Bell, for the Houses of Parliament, was made by J. Warner and Sons, 1856, under their Patent.

Patent Church, Turret, and Alarm Bells, of all sizes, at per pound. Old Church Bells Recast, or taken in exchange.

Galvanized Iron Tub GARDEN ENGINE, with Warner's Registered Spreader, is strongly recommended for durability and low price, viz., £2 19s., to hold 10 gallons. Larger sizes can be had, in either wood or iron. Also Warner's Swing Water-Barrow, to hold 40 gallons, £3 3s.

May be obtained of any Ironmonger or Plumber, in town or country; or of the Patentees and Manufacturers (as above).

WILLIAM BOX,

𝔊𝔞𝔰 𝔉𝔦𝔱𝔱𝔢𝔯, 𝔅𝔯𝔞𝔰𝔰 𝔉𝔦𝔫𝔦𝔰𝔥𝔢𝔯, 𝔅𝔯𝔞𝔷𝔦𝔢𝔯,

AND BELL HANGER,

BROOK STREET, NEAR FRODSHAM STREET BRIDGE,

CHESTER.

Chandeliers, and every description of Gas Fittings supplied,
and neatly repaired on the shortest notice.

BRONZING AND LACQUERING

DONE ON THE PREMISES ON REASONABLE TERMS.

REPAIRS EXECUTED IN ALL THE VARIOUS BRANCHES.

𝔅𝔯𝔦𝔡𝔢 𝔈𝔞𝔨𝔢 𝔐𝔞𝔫𝔲𝔣𝔞𝔠𝔱𝔲𝔯𝔢𝔯

BY   T.O
APPOINTMENT   THE QUEEN.

RICHARD BOLLAND,

CONFECTIONER,

EASTGATE ROW, CHESTER,

Successor to the late Mrs. Thomas.

(NO OTHER PERSON HAVING THE PURCHASE AND USE OF HER
RECEIPTS FOR THE MANUFACTURING OF BRIDE CAKES.)

𝔚𝔢𝔡𝔡𝔦𝔫𝔤 𝔅𝔯𝔢𝔞𝔨𝔣𝔞𝔰𝔱𝔰

FURNISHED IN WHOLE OR PART.

PIC-NIC PARTIES SUPPLIED.

FRENCH AND ORNAMENTAL CONFECTIONERY.

Parties visiting Chester will find his Refreshment Rooms replete with
Soups, Pies, Jellies, Ices, and Pastry in variety.

List of Suscribers to the 1996 Edition

Elizabeth Allen – Chester
Curt Anstey – Chester
Klaus Armstrong-Braun – Broughton
Lawrence Asbury – Birkenhead
John Asbury – Birkenhead
Sue Atkinson – Chester
Mr & Mrs J H Bailiff – Chester
Mr Martin Bailiff – Chester
Mr Ian Bailiff – Chester
Barbara Banks – Chester
B D Bate – Chester
Patricia J Beevers – Little Thornton
David Alston Bell – Birkenhead
F G Betteridge – Acton Bridge
Polly Bird – Chester
Bishops High Library – Chester
Tony Bland – Tarvin
Mr & Mrs T S Bradbury – Oldham
Mr & Mrs H Bradley – Tarvin
Mrs P M Brannon – Chester
Terence Broadhurst – Cheadle
Brynteg Library – Wrexham
R J Burke B.E.M – Wrexham
Valerie Burnett – Upton
Mr A K Carsley – Knutsford
Ann-Marie Carvell Nee Paulson – Port Sunlight
D Charlton – Chester
Cheshire County Council Libraries and Archives – Chester (8)
University College of Chester Department of History (2)
Chester Youth Hostel
Chester Cathedral Library

A M G Churton – Chester
Peter Clark – Helsby
Geoff Clegg – Pensby
K G P Clemence – Chester
John Cockroft – Nantwich
R G Coles – Chester
Dr A E Comyns – Chester
James Cooper – Chester
G R Coppack – Rhuddlan
John Crawford – Chester
Jane Cresswell
Rae & Kathy Cross – Chester
Mrs E J Davies – Chester
J M Davies – Chester
R Davies – Isle of Man
St Deiniol's Library – Deeside
Bryan Dearden – Cuddington
J Derrick Leach – Newcastle-under-Lyme
Dr & Mrs J Dewing – Chester
Roy & Margaret Dixon – Tarvin
Bob Dobson – Blackpool
S J Donnison – Guilden Sutton
Denys T Doxat-Pratt – Chester
Colin Doyle – Chester
Duddon St Peters School – Tarporley
Miss J Dyson – Chester
Mrs Pat Eccleson – Upton
David John Edge – Irby
Lilian Edwards – Chester
David Evans – Conwy
Ann & Donal Farrell – Chester
C S Foden – Chester
E A Foden – Chester

Les Foden – Broughton

Michael A Fleming – Chester

Gary Furness – Broughton

M N Gaskins – Dunstable (3)

Ronald S Gerrard – Milnthorpe

Robert Gray – Wrexham

Vic Groom – Chester

Brenda Groom – Chester

Grosvenor Estate – Chester (2)

Mr Christian M Gunther – Chester

Mr Sebastian M Gunther – Chester

Dr Michael M Gunther – Chester

Mr & Mrs J Gunther – Chester

M Gwynne-Jones – Chester

Walter Hamilton – Albrighton

Nigel Hardman – Upton

Mrs N A Haworth – Tarporley

David Hayns – Chester

Peter & Sheila Hebblethwaite – Chester (3)

Mr Peter M Hebblewhite

Christopher Matthew Riley

M H O Hoddinott – Chester

John Hubball – Hemel Hempstead

P M Hughes – Sale

J S H Huxley – Bordon

L Ingham – Whitby

Eileen Jeffery – Chester

R Jeffries – Chester

Jet of Deva – Chester

Dr S D John – Chester

B Jones – Chester

Miss June I Jones – Wrexham

K C Jones – Chester

T Kavanagh – Chester

Stephen Langtree – Chester

Frank A Latham – Alpraham

Derek Lawson – Chester

George E Lees – Holyhead

J B Lewis – Chester

John Lindop – Duddon Common

K E Little – Chester

W Mark Lloyd – Rossett

J H & D M Lloyd – Chester

R M C Logan – Chester

Mrs Janet Lowe – Chester

Joe Lupton – Connahs Quay

George & Joan Marsh – Radlett

Dr Geoffrey Martin – Chester

Dr Rosemary Martin – Chester

Mrs Pamela Mee – Liverpool

Ronald C Meakins – Chester

P & K Miles – Tarvin

Mrs R Milton – Chester

Len Morgan – Chester

Mr C M Morris – Chester

Mr Ray Mulligan Chester

Wendy McIntyre – Chester

J R Needham – Chester

Mary Norcott – Cadishead

Mrs P M Parry – Chester

Jack Pearson – Tattenhall

Mary Perrin – Sealand

R Pickering – Chester

D Pittaway – Ewloe Green

Mr & Mrs C Poage

M A Pollard – Chester

Mrs M A Price – Abergele
Mrs Patricia A Pritchard – Chester
W N Pritchard – Chester
Mike & Joy Procter – Chester
Dr A V Pullin – Chester
The Queens School – Chester
E A Rands – Chester
Harry Reynolds – Chester
R E Reynolds – Saltney Ferry
Miss G M Rhoden – Chester
Christopher Matthew Riley
Mrs Joyce Rimmer – Chester
Alec Robertson
E A Robinson – Rochdale
Gerald Roose – Chester
John Ross – Chester
Wm.A.Rowland – Chester (2)
Frank Rowlands – Chester
Mr & Mrs S H Rowlands
John Rowley M A, R.I.B.A
David C Russell – Chester
Valerie Salisbury – Helsby
John Saville – Wallasey
C A Shadbolt – Broxton
Mr & Mrs D J Shannon – Warrington
John Sheldon – Chester
Stewart & Linda Shuttleworth – Chester
Yvonne Siddle – Chester
Melanie Simcock
Eileen Simpson – Duddon
Anita Slater – Wallasey
Janet Smith – Heswall
South Cheshire Family History Society – Crewe

174   C B Spurgin, MA,C Phys,F.Inst.P – Sleaford

Maureen M Stanley – Chester

Eric Stapley FCA – Chester

J K Stinson – Chester

Arthur Stockdale – Old Colwyn

Mr R Stones – Malpas (2)

Jean Tarbuck – Chester

Mr D F Taylor – Wallasey

G Taylor – Chester

Richard & Barbara Thake – Toronto, Canada

Roy & Ann Thomason – Chester

Mr J R Todd – Tarvin

Richard Vaughan-Davies – Mold

John Venables – Chester

R M Vokes – Chester

C H Walker – Chester

Mrs E M Walker – Chester

Bernard A Wall – Chester

Miss S J Warne – Middlewich

Mrs Jean M Webb – Cheadle

Dr & Mrs G B White – Chester

Mary Wicks – Chester

K R Wilderspin – Chester

D Willcocks – Chester

Mr P F J A Williams – Chester

Mr Ian D Williams – Chester

John H Williams – Chester

Mrs Sarah Willis Nee Bailiff

Harold Wilson – Chester

Eileen Willshaw – Chester

Mrs J A Winepress – Farndon

John L Wolfenden – Chester

N B Wright – Tarvin